Storylines & Storytelling

What They Remember
and Repeat

WHAT BUSINESS EXECUTIVES HAVE TO SAY
ABOUT SALLY WILLIAMSON

"In Storylines & Storytelling, Sally Williamson provides a framework for leaders to connect to the hearts and minds of employees, customers and community members. Sally not only provides a road map for telling impactful and inspirational stories but also motivates leaders to lead authentically with presence and poise."

Candice L. Saunders
President and CEO
Wellstar Health System

"Great communication touches emotions. It can change minds and move people to action. Great communication starts with storytelling. Sally takes the mystery out of telling stories and can help move you from being a competent speaker to a compelling one."

Russell Weiner
Chief Operating Officer
Domino's

"Sally and her team are masters at teaching communicators how to connect on a human and emotional level. Her three-step formula has the right ingredients to make your points memorable and actionable, and you'll find great value in her insights whether you're talking to 1000 people or to your team."

Laura Wilbanks
Chief Marketing Officer
Equifax

"Sally Williamson knows how to capture the customer perspective in every storyline. Originally collaborating with her as a young sales leader, she had noticeable and measurable impact on my business and how we differentiated ourselves in the market. She is definitely the expert when striving for compelling conversation with your customers and sales teams."

Bill Hampton
SVP, GM Financial Institution Services
Worldpay

"I've known Sally for more than a decade, and I value her ability to turn details into a storyline that listeners want to hear. It takes discipline, creativity and the tools that she shares through hundreds of workshops every year. Sally will change the way you talk to your customers and the way your customers talk to you."

Kermit Randa
Chief Growth Officer
Waystar Revenue Cycle Technology

"Sally is an expert at crafting a powerful story that's easy to follow. She can prepare any communicator for any format or audience, and she gives you the framework and the confidence to always achieve your desired results."

Pedro Cherry
EVP, Customer Service & Operations
Southern Company

Storylines & Storytelling

What They Remember
and Repeat

Sally Williamson

Published by Sally Williamson and Associates, Inc.

Two Buckhead Plaza

3050 Peachtree Rd NW, Suite 400

Atlanta, GA 30305

ISBN 987-0-9837069-1-5

Library of Congress Control Number: 2018902410

DEDICATION

To the storytellers in our past who shaped memories.....
......the storytellers in our lives who paint possibilities....
..and the storytellers in our future who will be great leaders.

Table of Contents

Section 1
Storytelling

1

Why Storytelling?

It's Thursday, 8am. Pretty early for someone who was up after midnight, but that's common practice at industry conferences and large company meetings, because colleagues and peers mingle late into the night— networking, reconnecting, and building relationships that will prove fruitful in the months ahead.

You're feeling a little sluggish as you head into the massive ballroom for the opening session, but the room is anything but tired. The pulse of the music is electric and infectious. A thousand audience members begin to fill the seats, their energy visibly rising with anticipation.

It's your first look at the conference setup and it's clear the coordinators have spared no expense. Screens wrap from one end of the massive stage to the other and splash light and color on the audience. The stage is set with sleek white leather chairs.

The bells and whistles are all in place. The music is interrupted as the host announces the conference will kick off in five minutes. You settle in with a fresh cup of coffee and high expectations, and begin perusing the conference app.

You might be surprised to know that the one person who is not as ready to go as the setting suggests is the senior leader. He's backstage passing off changes to visuals and skimming the teleprompter script over the operator's shoulder to ensure that he has remembered every detail. When the host announces that the conference is about to start, he moves toward the back steps and waits for his cue to join the MC on stage.

He steps up to the podium and launches into a keynote that covers the company's plans for the year ahead, calls out the trends that he is betting on and the big wins they expect, and then unveils some new concepts that customers can expect to see soon.

This isn't what you were hoping for. The dynamics of the room promised energy and entertainment—something memorable. But within the first five minutes of his speech, the energy in the room evaporates. You hear the details, but you don't really feel moved by them. The speaker clearly doesn't either. He's reading sound bites off a screen on the floor and seems to be working harder to read it right than to say it well.

What's worse, he's not saying anything you didn't already hear at his competitor's conference last month. You mentally check out and scan the app to see what's coming next.

The second speaker is Julie, a senior manager on the strategy team. You don't know much about her, but the topic intrigues you so you resolve to be patient and see if the energy changes. You slouch a little further into your seat and skim through emails until the keynote wraps up.

After what feels like an eternity, the speaker winds down and the MC brings back the energy with audience participation and the highly charged music returns. You adjust your posture as the MC announces the next speaker.

Julie's posture is different from the moment she walks out. No slides appear behind her. She seems completely at ease as she scans the room and begins to tell a story about an experience she had six months ago at a conference just like this one. She expresses exactly how you felt this morning after the late-night networking and early morning call for caffeine. In short order, she makes you feel as if she knows how you are feeling at that exact moment.

From there, she seamlessly transitions into why certain strategy insights can reset the direction of managers just like you.

If you weren't so engrossed in her talk, you might notice that you've shifted forward in your seat and begun to listen with a whole new level of attention. In fact, the whole audience looks rapt. She's funny, witty, and at total ease with what she's saying and what she wants you to get out of it. Julie's not just a speaker; she's a storyteller.

Instead of listing evidence to prove her point, she leads a room of 1,000 listeners on a journey to show why competitors collaborate and innovations that she believes will change the marketplace. She weaves in industry examples and insights, but she never wavers from the journey. It's clear where she wants to take you and, like every other listener in the room, you gladly go along for the ride.

Her presentation ends the way it started—back at the conference she attended six months ago. She takes a long pause, nails a closing tagline, and walks off the stage.

The lights come up, and everyone looks around. You overhear some audience members talking about the examples she shared and others talking about her. You can tell that others are thinking the same thing you are: it's an interesting idea. It's worth considering. Who in this room could make a difference in my business?

What you don't hear is any mention of the CEO of the company who was the opening keynote speaker. His remarks were forgotten the moment they were spoken.

The speaker's impact isn't because she's a well-paid professional speaker. It's because Julie knows how to connect to people through storytelling. She's a compelling communicator…and you will hear her name time and time again as her career advances.

There is a difference between a competent communicator and a compelling one. We don't just look for the storytellers once a year at the industry conference. We hope for them in every meeting, on every conference call, and in the monthly town hall meetings.

Stories make information relevant, relatable, and applicable to what we do. They make it easier to pass along strategies and inspire others to get on board with changes or a new focus. And yes, we like to be entertained as we process all the information coming at us.

Storytelling is one of the oldest forms of communication known to mankind. Cavemen drew stories on walls; Egyptians depicted them in hieroglyphics. Before written history, cultures used stories to pass their customs from one generation to the next. Religious and political leaders have always used stories to build a following.

Stories are the common thread that link us to what has already happened and what is still to come.

Stories throughout history have been able to make great things memorable. We remember that:

- Columbus sailed the ocean blue in 1492...and started American history.

- Santa Claus leveraged the nose of a reindeer...and delivered presents on a magical night.

- The tortoise outran the hare...and taught us that slow and steady wins the race.

- Martin Luther King pulled all of us into a dream...and we can still hear it today.

- Scarlet O'Hara told us to "Think about it Tomorrow"...and helped us see hope in devastation.

- Rocky Balboa turned a boxing match...into a theme song for every physical challenge.

Through parables and fables, novels and ballads, all of us have learned lessons and shared them with others. Chances are you can trace many of your life values back to stories.

Yet somewhere along the way, communicators stopped using stories in business settings. That's where our story picks up. As we did our research into the impact of storytelling in business settings, we were hit with a surprising truth: few business people use stories in their communications. Our research uncovered any number of reasons:

- Some say storytelling places a higher expectation on a communicator......(it does).

- Some question whether storytelling is appropriate in business...................(it is).

- Most say telling stories requires animation and vulnerability....................(it does).

- All say that storytelling has a clear pass/fail effect on a group...................(it can).

Maybe that's why it isn't always easy to find great storytellers in the business world. Cultures that have storytellers lean heavily on them to set vision, drive influence, and empower others to bring their best talents forward. Our research participants thought that most storytellers are leaders. But the truth is, there are storytellers all over organizations. They just aren't good at it yet. But they can be.

Storytelling starts with a basic concept. The role of communication is simple and difficult.

Communication occurs when the speaker's intentions connect to the listener's needs and interests.

If you've ever presented to a distracted team or disenchanted audience, you understand the difficult part of communication. This is why most people aren't likely to take the risk of adding storytelling to an already stressful situation.

Communicators understand the power of the listener, but they don't always understand the interest. They're told, "Be direct and get to the point," and they take it to heart. It's true that communication has to be clear, but our research shows that listeners also want those thoughts to connect to each other. They prefer thoughts be woven together rather than listed point-by-point.

In our exploration of storytelling, the listener will be front and center because the more it is understood how others respond to communication the easier it is to deliver on those expectations.

At some point, you might wonder if storytelling is an art or a science. The truth is, it's a little of both. In our workshops, we teach the science and structure of the storyline and we also teach the art of engagement—how to pull listeners in.

In the chapters ahead, you'll read about both the art and the science of storytelling. You'll also read insights from listeners about what makes information memorable and repeatable. You'll read stories—of course!—about how managers and leaders have developed their storytelling skills over time.

But ultimately, I hope the book will inspire you and your ability to become a great storyteller.

2

The Listener's Perspective

One of the questions I hear at the midpoint of a workshop or coaching engagement is: "How do you know so much about our business?" There are some fields that we know pretty well, but for the most part what we tell people is: it feels like we know your business because we know your listeners.

At other times I hear, "You don't know our business well enough to help us with this." My response is always the same: "It's your job to know your business. It's my job to know your listener."

To better understand the impact of communication today and people's appetite for stories, we conducted a third-party survey across our client base and focus groups with our workshop participants.

We wanted to understand the listeners' perspectives, and we asked about takeaways, challenges, and overall impressions in a business setting. When we measured the effectiveness of communication, the results weren't pretty. This level of frustration is something that every communicator should sit up and take note of.

We wear listeners out. There is a dichotomy in our lives as listeners. On the one hand, there has never been so much creativity in how people capture our attention. From videos to songs, Facebook to Instagram, we capture impressions and we love it! We experience stories across different platforms and stories keep evolving in different formats. We're constantly telling stories and following stories, and we remain captivated by stories.

Then we go to work. We're asked to sit in meetings, presentations, and conference calls. Some people do this at least twice a day; some do it all day. The presentations aren't short, they aren't expressive, and listeners are exhausted by them.

Our research shows that 60% of listeners go to presentations and meetings and are unsure of what they will be asked to do with the content or how they are expected to participate in the discussion. In fact, 30% go further and say they don't even know why they were invited, what topic is being discussed, or who the presenter is. How can this be?

At a time when businesses are so focused on their customers' voice and personalizing every aspect of marketing, why are most presentations and meetings so bland?

Listeners say that presentations are hit or miss. They're rarely memorable, and they are frequently too long. Presentations are rarely entertaining or enjoyable and at least half of them are a waste of time. Yikes!

And while our attention spans are short, as listeners we'd prefer a presenter who is a great storyteller and who takes time to develop a storyline on a topic than someone who is brief and factual. That's surprising since the feedback that many presenters get is, "You need to get to the point; you're too long winded."

That's probably accurate feedback. We've worked with many communicators who ramble and just can't seem to make their point clearly. It's more than that, though. What listeners really want to know is what's the point and where is the storyline going…and then they are more than willing to join the presenter on the journey, if the journey itself is entertaining enough to hold the listeners' attention.

According to my conversations with listeners, business communicators need to use stories to make content more memorable and repeatable. It's a tall order because telling stories takes confidence and physical effort to animate a story in a way that listeners find entertaining and engaging.

Most of the time, listeners' expectations are not met. Only 22% of interviewees regularly hear stories that they consider memorable. And, the same group said that stories would be more memorable if the presenter were a better storyteller and if the stories aligned better to the topic. It isn't just about entertaining. It's about connecting. It takes work to align stories to storylines in a way that renders the content personal and relevant.

Even if a speaker accomplishes all that, it may not be enough. Everyone has encountered a great communicator who told a memorable story…but then no one ever repeated it or applied it. Doesn't that defeat the point of storytelling?

Stories are meant to be memorable and repeatable. Only 18% of listeners say that they repeat stories that they hear in a business setting. That's a stark contrast with how often we repeat stories in our personal lives. Most people can't wait to share stories that they relate to or learn from. Why isn't this the case in business? Listeners surveyed offer three reasons: the stories have to (a) connect with their own lives and objectives, (b) involve some emotion from the storyteller, and (c) preferably contain an element of surprise. That's a lot to ask of already-busy communicators. It's little wonder most settle for competence rather than connection.

People who like to tell stories usually say that storytelling comes naturally for them. It helps them connect with an audience and drive a point home. People who don't tell stories say it makes them uncomfortable because they don't have the polished presentation skills. They worry that a story will fall flat and not connect with the listeners. They think it's difficult to find stories that are relevant to their business.

It sounds as if there's no middle ground: either a person is a born storyteller or they're not. But there should be a middle ground. That's the reason for this book and for the storylines and storytelling workshops we run. Storytelling isn't a skill that is reserved for those who are born with it. It's a skill that every communicator can embrace and leverage to connect listeners to business content.

The challenge in business communications is that listeners are bored because the content is dry. People drift off in meetings and don't understand the call to action. The answer is clear, but challenging: to make the content relevant, make it interesting. Listeners want stories. Our research suggests that they also need stories.

3

From Information to Communication

When I meet with someone to help structure an upcoming presentation, I always ask these three questions:

- What do you want the listener(s) to hear?

- What do you need the listener(s) to believe?

- What do you expect the listener(s) to do?

The questions are pretty basic, but presenters often find it difficult to answer them. That's because few presenters start with the listener. They can tell me a lot about what they want to say and they have reams of data and insights on ways that they can say it. The problem with this strategy is that it doesn't begin with the end in mind. If a speaker doesn't have a clear idea of what the listener should take away, then chances are good the presentation will not have a lasting impact.

The listeners' feedback outlined in Chapter 2 suggests that they have low expectations for takeaways. I think this is because most communicators set low expectations for themselves, often without knowing it.

Years ago, I worked on a technical presentation with a seasoned and respected senior manager in a global engineering firm. We worked hard to simplify the concepts and connect the storyline, but it wasn't easy. To be honest, I got a little frustrated with how disjointed the content was and the level of detail he was determined to include. It felt like we'd solve one weak point only to get to the next one.

Every time I asked him about the listener, he would dismiss my questions and tell me "not to worry so much about that." An hour in, we took a break. When we reconvened, I decided to get a little more direct.

The project itself was interesting, so I asked him to tell me more about the team and the initiative. I discovered that he was leading one of the largest projects to come out of his firm in the last three years. We were developing a presentation for 200 engineers who were all working on different steps of a complex design, yet there was nothing in his content that connected these 200 people to each other.

I posed one of the key questions mentioned at the beginning of this chapter: "What do you expect the attendees to do with this information?" His response? "I don't have any expectations of these listeners. I was asked to overview the project and that's what I'm going to do. I'd like to show up, push out the details, and then let them get to work."

Now there was something to work with.

I shared my perspective on listeners and why they don't like to have information pushed at them. I asked him: if his role was to "push out the details," then who was going to set the vision for this project? Who would make everyone in the room feel connected to each other and to a project that had the potential to shift their entire industry? What would be the story about this project that they would tell their friends and families and colleagues for the next three years, and who would give them that story?

We were making progress.

He said that he had no idea, but he didn't think it was his role. He agreed that it would be much more interesting and rewarding to work on a project that had a clear vision wrapped around it. But as a communicator, he thought his responsibility stopped at conveying information. If anybody was going to deliver a vision, it should be the CEO, not him.

I then asked if the CEO of the firm went around and launched every initiative within the company. He started to get it.

Now, this guy wasn't a novice. He gave presentations frequently, and they were always heavy on details. He thought people listened to him, but he didn't know what stuck and he rarely got feedback.

The most revealing thing he said was: "Honestly, it's a lot of work to show up and share information. If I have to start thinking about what people do with the information, I will be overwhelmed."

At that point, we reached the real focus of coaching: to help him simplify his process and build storylines with the listener in mind. As he took my coaching to heart, he told me that it totally changed the way he thought about his role as a communicator.

I've heard similar comments many times, and it gets to the root of the communication challenge.

All employees want relevant information and compelling ideas. They want to align to the communicators, and strategies moving the company forward, but they can't align if the ideas aren't built and presented with them in mind.

Companies are full of competent communicators who see their role as informants. There is never a shortage of information being said, but there seems to always be a shortage of concepts that are being heard.

In order for information to have value, communicators have to prepare with the listener in mind.

Companies don't always talk about their internal communication flow, but this is a critical part of getting all levels of leaders to think about responsibility. When we lead this discussion, we intentionally oversimplify it, as shown in the diagram below, to help people conceptualize communication flows.

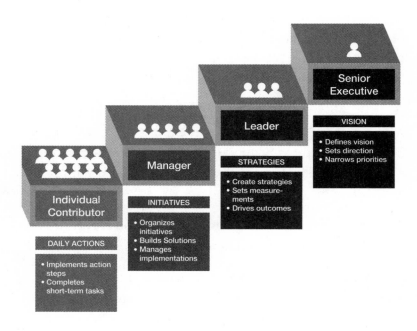

Of course, it's never as clean and simple as the diagram shows. Communication gets messy. Everyone needs to feel that they have a role and a responsibility to keep communication going. In order for communication to have impact, each level has to connect to the others around it.

Most senior-level executives get this. They have a clear communication plan and are intentional and consistent about the cadence and tone of the messages they deliver. If you listen to a well-written keynote, you'll notice the speaker moves from the broadest of strategies to a personal thought about the individuals in the room. Senior leaders don't stop in the middle with the structure of how things get done.

The sticking points in most companies are typically at the level of manager or director where presenters either leave gaps in communication or they step all over each other in how they frame ideas. Like in the story above, some get mired in details and others never really tell their employees how it impacts them or what their role will be. Few at this level ever anchor their thoughts back to the broader vision or strategy of the company.

When I challenge people on this, the most common response is: "All employees know that. They've already heard it." The feedback we looked at in Chapter 2 suggests otherwise.

Most employees aren't hearing the message even if it has been said multiple times. If they've heard it, they weren't really sure what to do with it or how to apply it to their work. And that leads us to the core elements that listeners value in communication.

4

Our Three Step Formula

When we ask listeners what it takes to influence people, they describe communicators who are confident, passionate, intentional, and authentic. These are the style elements of a storyteller, and we'll talk about these attributes in chapters 21–24. When we ask listeners what parts of a presentation they plan to repeat, they talk about clarity, sound bites, and how the communicator made them feel about an idea at the time.

I'm reminded of a quote I heard years ago about why people follow leaders:

"We value integrity, but we follow clarity."

It's so true! This is why leaders and managers with the best of intentions don't always get heard. It's also the reason storytelling is more complicated than it may initially seem.

A few years ago, I was called for jury duty. I respect civic duty, but two weeks away from the office can wreak havoc on a small business. Once I got over the hassle and lost revenue, I realized that I had a front row seat for a lesson on human behavior and storytelling.

This trial was a personal injury case. Without exception, the jurors felt sorry for the plaintiff and disliked the defense attorney, who came across as insensitive. And yet, the defense attorney did one thing very well. From the opening remarks, he positioned a message about intuitive steps and personal safety. He connected with the jurors on what people instinctively do to test water temperature. He even used his hand to act it out, and the gesture (and associated story) stuck.

Each time we gathered in the jury room, someone brought the gesture and the story up. it. It became a point of levity for the group because we all knew it and could mimic it. Thanks to this gesture and his carefully formulated communication, his storyline was memorable and repeatable.

Here's the interesting part. When we reached deliberation, the gesture became more than a mimic. Think about it: we'd been inundated with facts and details. The prosecuting attorney had taken us deep into the weeds, rattling off detail after detail. He did use examples, but it was a challenge to remember and connect all of them. We were short on takeaways. What resonated was the defense storyline. As a jury, we followed clarity, and in the end, the defense attorney won the trial, and I can still remember the storyline to this day.

So, how did the defense attorney win the case? And more importantly, how can his tactics be used in a business context to "win" at communication?

The defense attorney had a clear storyline. He knew where he wanted to lead his audience, and he navigated each step of the trial with the intention of moving the jury toward his destination. His point was clear, and he reinforced it in multiple ways.

His style had an impact as well. Even though we didn't initially like him because we thought he was insensitive, his style proved to be consistent with how he felt about the evidence in the trial. As a storyteller, he created interest, energy, and conviction behind his evidence and his beliefs about the case.

And, he used stories throughout the evidence to validate his beliefs. He didn't go deep into details or the science behind his evidence. Instead, he made his evidence relevant to everyone with stories and examples that the jurors could easily relate to.

So, was it the power of the story that made us act on his presentation or was it the power of the storyline? Did we value the story itself or how the communicator told-it?"

It's actually all three.

Our formula for compelling communication is:

A clear storyline + memorable stories + a compelling storyteller

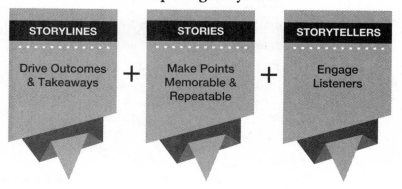

The storyline is the secret sauce. It's a framework for the flow of ideas. Specific stories are tied to specific points within the storyline. In order to inspire action, great communicators have to start with a measurable impact and message, and then learn to develop a storyline that proves it out.

We talk about communication as a journey, and we teach people to lead the listener to a defined destination. That destination is the desired outcome: what listeners will do with what they've heard. The message has to be compelling, and it has to align with a need or priority for the listener. The storyline itself is what glues it all together. The storyline helps stories link to points and then points prove out the message. Chapters 5–6 will explore this further.

Organization is key. I've seen many techniques designed to help presenters organize their thoughts. Some communicators show me a bubble technique that puts each point inside a circle and then the communicator connects the circles to find the storyline path. Others use an illustration that resembles a tree wherein the main point is the trunk and other ideas branch off of it. Some use trigger words to connect a list of ideas. All of these techniques are about linear connections. They build from the details to help the communicator jump from one point to the next. In order for the material to be memorable, the listener would have to write each point down and try and recreate the speaker's methodology. That's a lot of work!

Instead, the real value of communication is that all of those points roll up into a clear storyline. Enter the storyline— the one compelling idea that all of the points validate. Listeners will rarely remember point after point. But they will remember a storyline and the message that holds it together. And when they do, they tend to latch onto a story or two that they'll repeat to commemorate the storyline.

Case in point: I've told my jury duty story several times to different groups. I rarely tell it the same way twice. Based on a group (or my memory!), I use different points or anecdotes to bring the experience to life. But part of the defense attorney's message never wavers. I've held onto his storyline and I associate different details of the experience when I repeat it in different contexts.

The goal can't be for people to repeat details. The focus should be on making sure the storyline is memorable and that you've used a few stories to make it repeatable. Every listener will validate how they bought into the storyline in a different way.

In fact, great presentations are a balance of data points and stories.

Finding that balance is hard. We've all sat through presentations that were entertaining. The presenters had wonderful energy and told great stories. In the end, the audience was more entertained than driven to action. We've also experienced the opposite. Presentations that had good data points, but too many facts and figures. After a while, they run together and confuse the takeaway.

Great stories can bring ideas to life, provide a clear vision, and build understanding. Proof points can validate outcomes, turn a hunch into fact, and predict measurable results. In memorable and repeatable communication, a listener gets both stories and proof points. Good data points align with the brain, and good stories align with the heart. The storytellers who can engage both head and heart have a much greater chance of getting results.

This book introduces concepts that engage both the head and the heart. It presents a methodology for organizing storylines and stories in order to elicit a response from the listener. The Book takes you through the three elements of storylines, compelling stories, and engaging storytellers. It offers structure for content and style concepts that bring a more involved and engaged storyteller into corporate settings.

Ultimately, when a communicator combines a strong storyline, compelling stories, and an engaging storyteller, great things begin to happen.

Section 2

The Science of Storylines

5

The Storyline

Listeners universally say that the best communicators seem conversational, comfortable, and authentic, and it leads to the following conversation in our workshops.

> Participant: "I want to come across like Sam. He's so conversational in front of a group. He's comfortable and at ease. He's honest and engaging, and he's like that in meetings as well. He doesn't seem to be tied to notes or his outline."

> SW&A: "Sam sounds like a great communicator. How do you think he does that?"

> Participant: "Well, I don't think it's preparation. I think Sam just speaks well."

> SW&A: "Did Sam have a point that he wanted you to believe?"

> Participant: "Yes, and I still remember it."

> SW&A: "Did Sam prove his point and did you believe it?"

> Participant: "I didn't at first because it's a different direction than we've taken in the past. But he convinced me when he told a story of two companies

who had made similar mistakes and how one of those companies shifted their strategy in a new direction similar to the one he was proposing. I know the company well, and it was easy to understand his proposed direction based on their experiences."

SW&A: "And you think Sam came up with that new strategy and his points to prove it without any preparation?"

Participant: "No, I guess not. I never thought about how he did it. It just seemed so easy. He was clear and easy to follow, and he made it seem less about details and more about his big idea. I guess it did take a lot of preparation to link it together so well."

You bet it did. The really good communicators work so hard at it that the final delivery can make it appear much simpler than it really is. The most compelling communicators are those with intention, and they use some mechanics repetitively. They've thought about what they want to say, and they have all the core elements that lead a listener to an outcome.

That's not easy. Today's listeners are tough. They don't approach business content fascinated about topics or anticipating outcomes. And unfortunately, that's because they seldom leave with much. Our research with listeners confirmed this. At best, listeners come to business meetings, video calls and presentations with little expectation. Most sit in business meetings, video calls, and presentations wondering: Why am I here? What is my role in all this?

Clear communicators start with an intentional outcome. The task of the presentation is to guide the listeners to that outcome—some new understanding, belief, or takeaway on a topic. This is what listeners are looking for: a clearly defined outcome. If it's a measurable one, all the better.

Before listeners join the journey, they need some framing elements that help them understand where the journey is leading and how the communicator plans to get them there. The framing isn't a heavy agenda or a two-page executive summary. It's simply about a minute or so of framing that gives them the roadmap for communication.

The storyline holds three core elements: the message, the framework, and the stories. The visual below shows these elements from the listener's perspective.

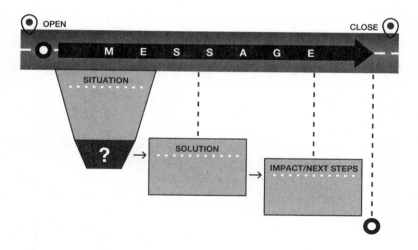

The Message frames the total journey. It is the headline of the storyline. It's a single statement that tells the listener what you want them to do and the value or outcome of doing it. (Chapter 6)

The Framework organizes the presentation material into three phases: Situation, Solution, and Impact/Next Steps. This division makes it easy for the listener to follow the journey and understand the intention behind the points that you're making. (Chapters 7–9)

The Stories are woven into the storyline. Stories add excitement, emotion, interest, and buy-in at key points along the journey. Where they're used depends on the storyline itself and where the communicator wants to add impact. (Section 3)

The storyline is the backbone of communication and yet often the most undervalued of all the concepts. This is because the listener doesn't perceive the storyline, and as illustrated by the conversation above, may not even realize that it's in place. Thus, using a storyline effectively is not something people pick up on merely by listening to a lot of presentations. It is something that must be learned. But it makes all the difference in a communicator who can relax and engage the listeners, because they have simplified the organization to one core message and three elements of a framework. They are working toward big transitions and not focused on presenting one point after another, which may cause them to miss a detail or lose their place.

It can easily happen if questions or comments from listeners derail their thoughts or they are given a reduced time commitment for their talk. The detail-by-detail presentation structure has little room for flexibility, since all of the points are in place and the presentation isn't complete without them. The framework above is built to easily flex to a change in timing or a question from the listeners. Since there are only three transitions in the journey, speaker and listener alike stay on track.

The science of communication organizes ideas in a way that makes them easy to deliver and easy to follow. A storyteller without a strong storyline may be entertaining, but they will seldom be repeated if they don't give their audience a clear takeaway.

6

Three Business Scenarios

So, let's consider three business conversations that could benefit from a clear and compelling storyline.

The three scenarios below reflect communication to employees and customers. This chapter will set up the scenarios. Subsequent chapters will use them as points of reference to discuss the elements of the storyline and the formula for telling stories.

These scenarios, selected from our training and coaching materials, are representative of several similar or hypothetical situations. We oversimplify to highlight the concepts rather than elaborate details. As a result, our scenarios are plausible but intentionally generic. Don't let the limited details or stretch on accuracy frustrate you.

SCENARIO #1: DATA SECURITY

Susan is a technology director whose responsibilities include data security protocol. To date, data security has been managed differently across seven divisions. Her company recently introduced a new analytics product, SmartLine, that leverages data across all of her divisions. The company expects to drive over $200 million in new revenue because of it.

But the program also creates new risks as data moves across divisions. With all the additional access points, Susan predicts the risk of a breach would increase by as much as 20%. The company needs a new enterprise protocol to cover these access points across all divisions before the analytics product launches. It won't be a welcome change because implementing the new protocol will disrupt the developers who are working to deliver the solution. Susan needs to recommend that all divisions halt development for 60 days to allow her to put a cross-divisional protocol in place.

What's the communicator's perspective?

Susan is probably worried that this project got ahead of protocol. She may feel like a policing officer, and in effect, she is. The company is excited about a transformational product and consequently put possibility ahead of responsibility. Now she's the one who has to blow the whistle and stall progress.

In a difficult position like this, we often see communicators trying to sugarcoat their recommendations. That's a dangerous strategy because if the concern isn't loud and the recommendation isn't clear, listeners are left with the impression that they may have other options—that the situation isn't really all that urgent. But in the months ahead, if the protocols don't hold and a breach occurs, this director will be held responsible. She needs to be as clear and assertive as she would be if the increased risk were confirmed at 20%. In the next few chapters, I'll illustrate how she does it.

SCENARIO #2: CHANGE IN MANAGEMENT

Bruce leads a large division of a communications company, and he is responsible for bringing a new bundle of sports programs to market. Sports programming drives viewership three times higher than other programming, so it is a critical part of revenue planning and growth strategies. But sports viewers don't follow providers; they follow events. It's hard to capture their loyalty through a subscription. Bruce's team has an exciting idea to build participation into the sports bundle and allow subscribers to engage with each other in something like a fantasy league for each event. They believe that this could increase subscriptions by as much as 50%.

However, Bruce doesn't have the capability on his team to develop this interactive feature. It will require someone with strong gaming experience and expertise in real-time technology. Bruce will have to get this in the marketplace within six months or he'll miss the sales opportunity. He needs to hire two seasoned professionals who can develop the product. This won't be well received by his team. They've worked hard to come up with the concept and assess its potential. Bruce has told his leaders about this, but it will be a culture shift for an organization that typically promotes from within. He needs to talk to the entire team about the urgency of innovating quickly and the opportunity to bring in diversity of thought and skills through new leadership.

What's the communicator's perspective?

I'd say Bruce feels torn between empathy and conviction. He knows he has the right idea to move his organization forward, but he doesn't want to lose his existing talent or the positive energy on his team. As with Susan in scenario #1, he has to communicate news that won't be welcomed by many in his group, and he will need to do so in a way that demonstrates he understands the feeling of disappointment. There is room for a forward-looking storyline that anticipates new opportunities for everyone as the outside talent helps them bring different products to market.

We use a similar example when we talk to leaders about moving from competent to compelling. This is more about the right emotional presentation than it is about the news itself. This leader needs to be open about his own struggle in reaching this decision. He would be wise to begin with a story of a time he was disappointed by a direction that didn't put him first.

Sometimes leaders present tough news too abruptly because they want to get it over with. They move too quickly to how things will be implemented before the audience really understands the need. It's important for this presenter to set the stage for the difficult news, helping his team understand why he's doing what he's doing, not just how he plans to do it. In the next few chapters, I'll reveal how to handle this.

SCENARIO #3: CUSTOMERS & PRODUCTS

Chandler is a salesperson for a start-up company, LoanLogic, that has developed an algorithm to qualify consumers for bank loans. It isn't a new concept. Financial institutions have several formulas to qualify loans. But LoanLogic has been able to bring personal analytics into the equation and can sync data from social media to profile people more effectively than a financial institution can.

Add to it a little sizzle and online interaction, and this tool may have great value to financial institutions who want to generate more loans. To prove the success of the algorithm and willingness of consumers to engage with the loan tool, LoanLogic set up smart kiosks in three shopping malls, positioned close to high-priced items like cars, jewelry, and electronics. The voice-activated kiosk drew a lot of attention and those who engaged the virtual loan officer completed the application process in under two minutes. The bank that piloted the kiosks with LoanLogic reported a 65% lift in loan applications and ultimately, a 50% increase in completed loans.

Chandler's next step is to get banks to purchase the product which can be applied to their website or in a free-standing kiosk like the one LoanLogic put in shopping malls. How will Chandler position the product?

What's the communicator's perspective?

This is a salesperson's ideal scenario, so Chandler is excited about the success of the kiosk pilot test and eager to position the product to financial institutions. It seems like an easy sell because the product works. It automates and simplifies what has traditionally been a manual, complex process, and it produces better results.

But of course, that's the communicator's perspective. In order to be successful with his prospects, Chandler will need to build a storyline that starts with their perspective. The most common blind spot we see in sales presentations is a focus on products and features instead of customer challenges and pain points.

As this storyline develops, Chandler will start with the consumer by discussing the traditional loan process versus the LoanLogic product.

Now the stage is set. We have three scenarios that illustrate common communication challenges and opportunities. As we'll see in the following chapters, the most important thing they can all do is begin their communication with a clear message that emphasizes the value to the listeners.

7

The Power of Messaging

If the storyline is the most undervalued element of communication, the message is the most valued. Listeners love it when they know what the speaker wants them to accomplish, and communicators tend to see outcomes when they start with a clear outcome in mind.

This critical element to communication is like the headline of the storyline. It's been called the common thread, the through line, the theme, the tagline, and the lead point. We call it the message to suggest that it is meant to be the takeaway or the repeatable benefit of the entire storyline.

The message is the make-or-break of effective communication because every listener wants to know: "What's the point?" When the speaker doesn't know, no matter how entertaining or interesting she may be, listeners aren't going to remember or repeat anything she said.

Listeners want messaging to be provocative, to set an expectation that needs to be explained or to commit to a value-driven outcome.

Most business communication should deliver measurable outcomes. When we build messaging into sales storylines, internal storylines, or conversations with leaders, we introduce a simple formula that aligns the communicator's ask with the listener's benefit:

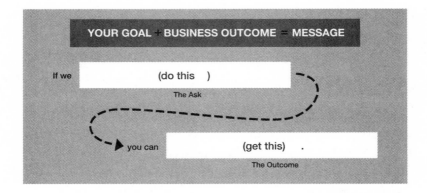

If we do this (the ask of the business), we will get this (a measurable business outcome.)

It's clear, it's concise, and the outcome is measurable.

The ask is an action or buy-in that has to be taken in order to reach the desired outcome. The outcome then helps the listener determine if the action is worth taking. Right away, the message defines the listeners' role—what they're being asked to do. They are then motivated to engage with the storyline in order to facilitate their decision.

Examples:

If we reallocate our resources, we can accelerate the product launch by 90 days.

By tailoring our message to a younger demographic, we will expand our visibility and improve leads by 40%.

By partnering with us as a data resource, you can segment your online campaigns and triple views of your virtual store this quarter.

A compelling message begins with the end in mind and sets the direction of the storyline clearly and early. In each of the messages above, it's easy to see what the listener is asked to believe or do and the value the communicator has placed on that action.

In my second book, *Leading Executive Conversations,* we share our research that confirms the value that leaders place on a measurable outcome. Over 97% of leaders surveyed said that a clear takeaway was the most important element of any communication.

The message shouldn't be confused with an overview or summary. It's a simple, bottom-line statement that defines the biggest takeaway or benefit. It isn't easy to develop, but it is well worth the time spent to balance simplicity and impact. The clearer the message is, the more likely it is to be heard and repeated.

In our programs, we've found that communicators rarely try to define the impact of their projects in a single sentence. When we ask them to do it, they struggle to express the value of the outcome and instead give us a laundry list of things they want the listener to do. They dilute their own message and add unnecessary layers of complexity.

Let's revisit the business scenarios from Chapter 6 and consider how messaging can help each communicator define the direction of the storyline.

SCENARIO #1: DATA SECURITY

Susan is a technology director whose responsibilities include data security protocol. To date, data security has been managed differently across seven divisions. Her company recently introduced a new analytics product, SmartLine, that leverages data across all of her divisions. The company expects to drive over $200 million in new revenue because of it.

But the program also creates new risks as data moves across divisions. With all the additional access points, Susan predicts the risk of a breach would increase by as much as 20%. The company needs a new enterprise protocol to cover these access points across all divisions before the analytics product launches. It won't be a welcome change because implementing the new protocol will disrupt the developers who are working to deliver the solution. Susan needs to recommend that all divisions halt development for 60 days to allow her to put a cross-divisional protocol in place.

Remember the communicator's perspective. Her attempt to be cautious might make the message too wordy.

If we move forward with the SmartLine launch as planned, without a cross-divisional security protocol, there's a chance that the additional access points that we created to enable analytics could increase our risk of a data breach.

If you say it out loud, you'll notice that her listeners are going to get lost in the details. It's a single sentence, but it includes too much detail. "There's a chance" will convince some listeners it will happen, but those who don't want to hear it will assume that it probably won't be an issue. And the listener has no real sense of the magnitude of the problem.

We would help this communicator get to a message along these lines:

If we delay the SmartLine launch for 60 days, we can adopt security protocols that will eliminate up to 20% added risk of a data breach.

The ask is clear: delay for 60 days. The impact is clear as well: eliminate the 20% increase in security risk. The listeners may not like it, but they clearly understand the ask and the outcome, allowing them to focus on the only important question: is a 60-day delay worth eliminating a 20% increase in security risks?

It won't be an easy decision, and the listeners will have to believe and accept the 20% risk increase and their options to protect against it. But it's clear where the storyline is headed. The communicator gave them a good focal point and should be able to pull them into the dialogue quickly.

SCENARIO #2: CHANGE IN MANAGEMENT

Bruce leads a large division of a communications company, and he is responsible for bringing a new bundle of sports programs to market. Sports programming drives viewership three times higher than other programming, so it is a critical part of revenue planning and growth strategies. But sports viewers don't follow providers; they follow events. It's hard to capture their loyalty through a subscription. Bruce's team has an exciting idea to build participation into the sports bundle and allow subscribers to engage with each other in something like a fantasy league for each event. They believe that this could increase subscriptions by as much as 50%.

However, Bruce doesn't have the capability on his team to develop this interactive feature. It will require someone with strong gaming experience and expertise in real-time technology. Bruce will have to get this in the marketplace within six months or he'll miss the sales opportunity. He needs to hire two seasoned professionals who can develop the product. This won't be well received by his team. They've worked hard to come up with the concept and assess its potential. Bruce has told his leaders about this, but it will be a culture shift for an organization that typically promotes from within. He needs to talk to the entire team about the urgency of innovating quickly and the opportunity to bring in diversity of thought and skills through new leadership.

Remember Bruce's perspective. He's ready to be direct about his message, but he could miss the opportunity to link the message to an outcome. He may be too tactical in defining what he's doing and not helping his team hear it as an action to drive an outcome.

In situations like this, we often hear communicators state an objective instead of a message.

I've hired two experienced gaming professionals to help us get the sports bundle to market.

Ironically, we would tell Bruce that this statement may actually be too direct. It will be heard as something he has done to his team rather than with them. It sounds tactical and doesn't represent a team outcome or benefit. We would suggest that he develop a message that talks about adding capability to the team. This way his storyline positions the need before introducing the new people who will fill it.

People and resources are a means to an outcome. He doesn't want the team to hear they're getting a new leader at the start of his storyline. He wants the team to hear that they need expanded capability because it suggests that his decision adds to their skills versus overriding them.

We would help this communicator get to a message like this:

By adding capabilities outside of our experience, we can launch a sports package that could double subscriptions in six months.

SCENARIO #3: CUSTOMERS & PRODUCTS

Chandler is a salesperson for a start-up company, LoanLogic, that has developed an algorithm to qualify consumers for bank loans. It isn't a new concept. Financial institutions have several formulas to qualify loans. But LoanLogic has been able to bring personal analytics into the equation and can sync data from social media to profile people more effectively than a financial institution can.

Add to it a little sizzle and online interaction, and this tool may have great value to financial institutions who want to generate more loans. To prove the success of the algorithm and willingness of consumers to engage with the loan tool, LoanLogic set up smart kiosks in three shopping malls, positioned close to high-priced items like cars, jewelry, and electronics. The voice-activated kiosk drew a lot of attention and those who engaged the virtual loan officer completed the application process in under two minutes. The bank that piloted the kiosks with LoanLogic reported a 65% lift in loan applications and ultimately, a 50% increase in completed loans.

Chandler's next step is to get banks to purchase the product which can be applied to their website or in a free-standing kiosk like the one LoanLogic put in shopping malls. How will Chandler position the product?

Chandler's perspective is one of excitement. He won't have a difficult message, but we worry that he may not have a message at all. Too often, sales meetings and presentations jump from "thank you for your time" to "here's how our product works." Remember that the salesperson needs to use messaging to frame a clear value and benefit to the customer.

We would help the salesperson get to a message like this:

By implementing our two-minute tool, you can increase loans by 50%.

This message is a good balance between what the salesperson wants and what the customer gets. The customer is drawn into the storyline by the promise of a clear and measurable benefit. As the conversation progresses, the customer will decide if a 50% increase is worth the cost of a new loan tool.

Sales presentations often wait until the end to get to the impact and results. But with customers, it's more compelling when a salesperson begins with the measurable benefit so that the customer can readily weigh the benefit against the costs or disruption of implementing a solution.

For any communication, there are multiple ways to frame a message. Our guiding principles are:

Keep it to one clear sentence. If the listener doesn't hear the message, there's no point having one.

Use the formula to marry an ask with an outcome. It's important for the listener to know what they need to do and what they will get out of it.

Add measurement to outcomes. Think how much, how long, how big, by when. Outcomes can be quantified by percentage, size, revenue, time, and more.

The goal is to launch the storyline with a clear direction and reason for the listener to engage in the presentation. And once the message is set, the listener is intrigued, and the storyline begins to unfold.

8

Framework Element: Situation

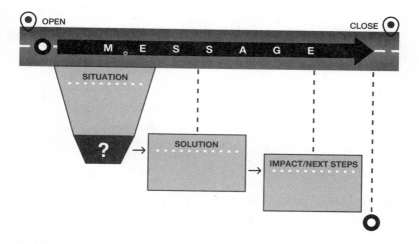

The visual introduced in Chapter 5 and shown above indicates three elements of the framework. There are two key things to notice.

First, the framework is intentionally simple. When we measured what people actually retain from presentations, we found that they remembered as little as 15%. A simple framework means that the listener isn't trying to hold onto 25 different points being pushed at them. They're following three big concepts along the storyline's journey. The framework has just two pivot points as listeners move from

Situation to Solution and then from Solution to Impact. This helps the listener hear transitions and it makes the order of thoughts much easier to follow.

Second, the Situation element seems different and sits higher than the others. That's intentional as well. The Situation represents the listener's perspective. Elevating the Situation signifies that the communication starts from the listener's perspective rather than the communicator's.

Too often, presenters jump into how to solve things, showcasing recommendations, timelines, and action plans. But listeners don't start with the how; they start with a desire to know what the presenter wants and why.

It seems simple, but it's hard for communicators to recognize this, since communication is usually driven by the need to solve something or bring recommendations and opportunities forward. The next chapter discusses this in greater detail.

The Situation frames context on a topic. It sets up a reason to change something or move something forward. It also provides the sound bites that are likely to be repeated. Some refer to Situation as background, but it is more important than that. It positions the topic in a way that helps the listener think about the need to change something or adjust to a shift in the market.

I'll describe the listener's perspective in each of the scenarios and then introduce a model to help presenters organize ideas in the Situation phase.

> ### SCENARIO #1: DATA SECURITY
>
> Susan is the technology director who needs to put protocol in place to support the new analytics product, SmartLine. It won't be welcome because it will delay development for 60 days, but its implementation will counter the increased risk of a breach.

We presented the communicator's message as:

If we delay the SmartLine launch for 60 days, we can adopt security protocols to eliminate up to 20% added risk of a data breach.

Susan has put a lot of time into studying how analytics are being pulled and has discovered that the firewalls have been compromised. She believes that her communication should start with what it will take to solve that problem. She's prepared to share the steps she has come up with and justify why she needs 60 days to implement the new enterprise protocol.

- The trouble is, the listener won't react well to a Solution-focused storyline, which skips over all of the listener's potential questions:
- Why would risks increase with smart technologies?
- What have other companies done about the increased risks associated with increased data?
- Why didn't you bring this up before we started developing SmartLine?
- What is our risk % today and how big of a deal is a 20% increase?
- Why do we have seven different protocols?

55

This storyline needs to start with context. What's different about this new technology and what are the best practices it requires? The listener will need to know what is currently in place, why the needs have shifted, and why the problem wasn't addressed when development began. The listener needs to see the need to do something different before the communicator talks through how to do the something different.

The listener's need for context is the most common blind spot that communicators have. We would encourage the technology director to frame the Situation with the following talking points.

DATA SECURITY SITUATION

- Consumers want products to share information and offer one consistent response.

- Smart technologies require products and solutions to share all they know.

- Companies have to build interfaces that allow their solutions to exchange information.

- Smart products need open architectures that we now know are up to 20% more vulnerable to data breaches.

- Our products were built on closed architectures, and we don't currently share data across divisions.

- We have minimal security threats because of strong firewalls unique to each division.

- SmartLine will leverage data across seven divisions.

- To build SmartLine, we removed the firewalls that protect data in each division.

- This increases access points for breaches and puts us at a 20% higher risk of exposure.

- We don't have an enterprise protocol in place because we haven't needed one until now.

- Can we develop an enterprise security protocol quickly to protect data from all divisions?

These talking points illustrate a clear challenge (increased security risk) and the need to overcome it. Let's look at the Situation in the change in management scenario.

SCENARIO #2: CHANGE IN MANAGEMENT

Bruce is responsible for a new bundle of sports programs. His team has laid the groundwork for an interactive tool that would allow subscribers to participate in each sporting event in a whole new way. But, the team doesn't have the experience necessary to design and manage the technology in real time. He needs to hire two industry pros to bring the idea to market, and he needs to let his team know about it.

We positioned the change in leadership with the following message:

By adding capabilities outside of our experience, we can launch a sports package that could double subscriptions in six months.

Bruce's storyline also needs to begin with the what and why instead of jumping into how the new team members will help get the product to market in six months. Working through his storyline, we would encourage him to start with the need to bring something new to market quickly and gain loyalty with subscribers. This is the heart of the storyline: the team has uncovered an opportunity to overcome a challenge that they've had for three years. It's hard, it's complicated and the sports customer is a tough one. If his team believes the challenge with subscriptions and wants to solve it, then it is easier to see how essential the new personnel are. Bruce can position the external hires as a necessary and desirable solution versus a sudden change that devalues the team's work to date.

We would frame the Situation in this scenario with the following talking points.

CHANGE IN MANAGEMENT SITUATION

- Sports programming drives three times the viewers of any other programming.

- Competition is fierce, as all content providers want to capture the sports enthusiast's wallet.

- Subscriptions are the best way to maximize sales, but sports viewers aren't typically interested in packages.

- Sports viewers like activities linked to pre-game and post-game shows and events.

- Research shows that viewers also participate in sports chat rooms and fantasy leagues.

- For the past three years, our subscriptions have produced minimal results.

- Sports enthusiasts haven't stopped viewing; they've shifted preferences based on offerings.

- Our team has a great interactive concept that could capture and retain viewers.

- It requires gaming sophistication to allow for sequencing and real-time interaction.

- We don't currently have this expertise on our team.

- Can we add resources to accelerate this concept and bring it to the marketplace in six months?

The talking points begin with marketplace challenges, then identify what the team has tried to do and why it's been difficult, to position a great idea without the tools to execute it. Again, the Situation helps the listener see the gap before the speaker proposes how to fill it.

Finally, the third scenario is the salesperson who wants to sell the loan tool to financial institutions.

SCENARIO #3: CUSTOMERS & PRODUCTS

Chandler is marketing a product designed to qualify consumers for loans. It's a new and innovative way to link personal data and social behaviors with financial information. The product was piloted in a shopping mall to see if the simple and quick process could drive up loan applications. It did. The pilot reported a 65% lift in loan applications and a 50% increase in completed loans.

We positioned the following message:

By implementing our two-minute tool, you can increase loans by 50%.

In this scenario, Chandler needs to start with the listeners' perspective and not rush ahead to describe product features. Here's how we would build the Situation for his storyline.

CUSTOMERS & PRODUCTS SITUATION

- Consumer behaviors and habits say a lot about what consumers value and how they spend money.

- Social media holds a lot of data about consumer activities and can predict spending patterns.

- Studies show that aligning with behavior on social media can lift sales as much as 40%.

- Financial firms look at what people earn and spend but don't have data on what people do.

- Loans are driven more by what people would like to do than what they actually do.

- Most online applications take five minutes to complete and applicants have to wait 48 hours for a reply.

- Financial institutions report a 45% incomplete rate on loan applications.

- The mall kiosk test positioned a financing option next to things that people would like to own.

- Voice-activation technology drove a conversation about behaviors, priorities, and choices.

- Algorithm linked interview responses with financial data for insights and assumptions.

- Kiosks drove higher levels of participation, increased leads, higher qualification rates, and increased sales.

- Can we help you increase loan applications and your loan closure rate?

Again, the storyline begins with insights on consumer behaviors derived from social media. It positions a concept and new data source that financial institutions may not have considered. It intrigues the listener by describing how the new data source is being leveraged and builds interest in a case study that proved it out. Since the listener is interested in what the presenter knows more than what he has to sell, that's a good starting place with customers.

While each of these storylines are different, they all begin by framing the Situation. The talking points move from broad contextualization and then drill down to an opportunity or problem to be solved. We call this technique funneling, and our model for the technique is below.

FUNNELING

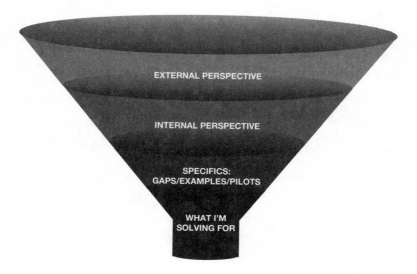

EXTERNAL PERSPECTIVE

INTERNAL PERSPECTIVE

SPECIFICS:
GAPS/EXAMPLES/PILOTS

WHAT I'M
SOLVING FOR

While the funneling concept flexes to fit different storylines, there are three basic levels to help the listener begin with a topic and an action or an opportunity that creates a reason for a Solution.

External Perspective: For most topics, the listener's connection starts outside their company with a trend or best practice in the marketplace. This is how the communicator can create timeliness and interest toward something that may be new or forward thinking.

In each of the scenarios, the talking points begin with an external change that could compel the company to rethink the way it does something.

- **Scenario 1**: This storyline starts with consumer interest in smart technology and the need for open architecture to deliver it.

- **Scenario 2**: This storyline begins with competition in sports subscriptions and looking for a way to build loyalty with these very profitable viewers.

- **Scenario 3**: This storyline positions the concept of uncovering consumer interest and activities to determine spending interest and priorities.

Each starting point is likely to solicit agreement or intrigue from the listener and that means the listener will follow the presenter to the next step in the communication journey.

Internal Perspective: The next level of the funnel moves from industry practice to the current circumstances of the company. In many cases, this level draws a comparison of where the market is headed and where the company is. It may mean looking at a desired future state in comparison to a current state, or a discussion of where the topic evolved from—how the company thought about it or acted on it in the past as opposed to its current stance.

- **Scenario 1**: We took down firewalls, thus removing the security layers we relied on in the past, in order to accommodate our new cross-divisional product.

- **Scenario 2**: We've been trying to increase subscription revenue for three years without results.

- **Scenario 3**: Loan applications don't look at behaviors and activities, and they take a long time to complete, so consumers frequently drop out of the process.

In each case, a gap is beginning to take shape between what could be and where we are today.

I call this a **Pivot in Belief.** It's the point at which most listeners take an interest in the storyline. The communicator has successfully introduced something the company could have and doesn't, or some possibility that the company isn't prepared for. The pivot point for the listener is usually something like "I didn't know that" or "I hadn't thought about that before."

The storyline has momentum, and the communicator has established credibility by introducing insights on a topic that the listener hasn't thought about. This leads listeners to consider: What challenges does this present for us? What do we have today if we don't have that? What are we missing?

Specifics: The "specifics" are the features of an existing program or the pain points and gaps caused by not moving toward the external perspective. Sometimes the specifics include an example or case study as in the sales story, or they may define a struggle that the company has overcome. If the topic is being introduced into the company for the first time, there may not be Specifics yet.

The specifics go a step deeper into context and help listeners understand the risks of not moving forward with whatever is being proposed. It is usually the specifics that create a sense of urgency or excitement around the topic.

- **Scenario 1**: We don't have enterprise protocol in place and increased access points associated with the new product put us at a higher risk of breach.

- **Scenario 2**: We have a great concept but not the right skill sets to build it.

- **Scenario 3**: We ran a pilot in a shopping mall and it drew interest and applications.

When the talking points are organized from External Perspective to gaps in the existing program, it leads the listener to ask: How can we solve this? How could we leverage this? In each scenario, we lead right to a question of how the gap could be solved or the opportunity could be leveraged. And, that's a great way to lead the listener to the desire to hear about a Solution.

The flow of the presentation is built with the listener in mind. That's how effective communication should work. Instead of starting with HOW something can be solved or what the communicator wants to do, these communicators were able to start with the listeners' perspective and create a need for a Solution which peaks the listeners' interest in hearing about a solution.

That's the first pivot in the storyline: getting from the Situation to the Solution.

9

Framework Element: Solution

By following the Situation–Solution–Impact model, the communicator is able to lead the listener from context to an interest in a Solution. Imagine the influence a speaker has when the listeners want to hear a solution, versus being in a position of trying to build interest with features, options, and timelines before the audience ever feels the need for any of it.

The Solution is no less important than the Situation; it just has to follow it. It is the communicator's priority and drives why the presentation or conversation is happening in the first place.

The Solution shows how things will happen and often includes more details than the other two elements. It is a recommendation or implementation. Be aware that while this is an important element, it is rarely where listeners pull repeatable sound bites, because solutions are more detailed and usually the responsibility of whoever is presenting them.

I've added talking points to support the Solution in each scenario. There are fewer talking points included in the Solution phase because I didn't add the details under each bullet. That doesn't mean that the Solution element is the shortest. In fact, it's often the longest because of the level of detail that communicators have under each bullet.

Scenario #1: DATA SECURITY SOLUTION

- Three options for enterprise security strategies
- Best practices from security vendors
- Vendor recommendation
- Implementation plan
- Development impact and timing options
- 60-day plan

The flow of this Solution begins with three options. Most listeners want to see some context for the leader's recommendation and how they arrived at their decision. It's impractical to lead a team through the full process, but a SWOT analysis, key metrics, or comparisons to other vendors can provide an effective and concise overview.

The development impact and timing options would be another place where Susan could give context for her decision. The assumption is that there are timing options, and those options may have been, for instance, 45 days, 60 days, and 90 days. The difference in timing could be based on how disruptive the enterprise solution will be to the network itself. This helps listeners see that other options were considered, but the middle ground seemed the best balance between quick results and adequate security measures.

Scenario #2: CHANGE IN MANAGEMENT SOLUTION

- Capabilities we need and how to get them
- Profiles of leaders who are joining the team
- How we will leverage their skills in six months
- What will shift in organization and responsibilities
- Big goals for six-month plan

The flow of this Solution starts with what the team needs. It builds from the Situation discussion of gaming and real-time interaction. The leader will start with capabilities needed and who has these capabilities in the marketplace. Ideally, he'll set up the kinds of companies that have great gaming tools and then link it to his announcement that he's hired leaders from those companies to join their team.

This demonstrates the need for the skills before introducing the people who possess them. We would encourage Bruce to focus on the projects and initiatives these leaders have been responsible for and to closely link their skill sets to results and projects that the employees have seen in the marketplace. This makes it easy for an employee to see the connection between what their team needs and the skill sets that are being brought in to meet those needs.

Scenario #3: CUSTOMERS & PRODUCTS SOLUTION

- The science of the LoanLogic algorithm
- Case studies of financial institutions
- Integration options: website vs. free-standing kiosks
- Timetable and expected costs

In the third scenario, the Solution begins with the science behind the algorithm. The listeners will want an explanation as to how the product works, and this allows the communicator to give a high-level explanation of the algorithm components and then illustrate the success of the tool through the presentation of three case studies.

Case studies are an intriguing part of a sales presentation because they act as stories inserted into the storyline and can be altered based on the needs of the prospective buyer. Each story reveals the challenge faced by a specific institution and how their tool helped in each case. We'll examine how such stories are developed in Chapter 19.

The choices or options in this presentation come later in the Solution discussion as Chandler presents different ways to integrate the algorithm into his clients' existing toolsets.

While the Solution carries details about how an idea or recommendation would be implemented, the talking points still flow from one idea to another. It's important to keep the storyline intact and not get bogged down in providing too much detail. Even though the Solution phase presents the communicator's perspective, the talking points should be organized based on the flow that makes sense to a listener. The communicator's ultimate goal is to keep the storyline moving forward.

When I help communicators build this element, I give them only one slide to represent each concept of the Solution. For example, one slide on Capabilities Needed, one slide for Vendor Options, one slide for Implementation, etc. This gives the listener a clear point at each step. Additional slides or details should only be added to help keep the talk track moving forward. If they pull the conversation too far off base or seem to derail the flow, then it is better to leave them out.

The talking points in the Solution engage the listener in decisions such as making a recommendation, hiring a vendor, or determining a timeline. Once the listener has confidence in the thought behind the Solution, most are ready to pivot a second time and see the Impact and Results proven out.

10

Framework Element: Impact/Next Steps

The Impact element of the storyline is the shortest and provides the proof points for everything presented. It is the end of the journey—the point at which the communicator proves the outcome promised in the message.

When the message is compelling, some listeners will jump in and ask about the outcome at the very beginning. It's important that communicators resist the temptation to jump ahead because the listener needs the Situation and Solution elements to buy into the proof points in the Impact.

That's why the message is so important. It offers a clear promise that connects the ask and the outcome. The message tells the listener where the talk track will end, and it creates enough intrigue that the listeners are interested to see the promise proven out.

The Impact element holds the proof points. There are often more proof points than the lead one that was framed in the message at the outset. But this section is never heavy because it narrows the Impact elements to the takeaways that are relevant to and valued by the listeners.

Let's look at how each of the scenarios wraps up.

Scenario #1: DATA SECURITY IMPACT

Susan's message was: **If we delay the SmartLine launch for 60 days, we can adopt security protocols to eliminate up to 20% added risks of a data breach.**

Susan has to prove where the 20% added risk comes from. She's already highlighted what has happened with other companies, but she needs to show key metrics in this element to help the group understand the full impact of the costs of exposure. She should also be prepared to show the costs of the 60-day delay. This puts both perspectives on the table for the listener to compare the risk of moving forward with the new technology and the potential costs associated with the delay.

Here are the talking points:

- Costs of exposure—magnitude of a breach to the enterprise
- Costs of 60-day delay
- Next step: buy-in with development teams
- Next step: hire vendor

It's a presumptive close because Susan also has next steps outlined and will be able to share what she needs to get buy-in from development teams and to hire the vendor. The Next Step demonstrates that she is ready to get to work quickly and it also helps the listeners complete the work. They will leave the presentation understanding the overall impact and the specific actions that their teams will undertake. The technology director may also have plans for how the new protocol will be communicated across divisions or may have others in the audience who take responsibility for communicating next steps.

Scenario #2: CHANGE IN MANAGEMENT IMPACT

In the second scenario, Bruce's message was:
By adding capabilities outside of our own experience, we can launch a sports package that could double subscriptions in six months.

In the Solution, Bruce shared his plan for adding new leaders and the changes it will require in the organization. He also set big goals for the six months ahead. In the Impact element, he wants to focus on the way that adding skills to the team will impact both the organization as a whole and the individuals sitting in the room. For most of his employees, this change is both a disruption and an opportunity. The six months ahead will mean a shift in their work roles and relationships. It will be fast, challenging, and disruptive, but it will also create new learning and direction going forward. It's potentially very exciting for employees to work on cutting-edge concepts and learn new skills related to gaming sequencing and real-time interaction—it just depends on how Bruce presents it.

Here are the talking points:

- What it will mean for our business
  * Innovative leaders
  * Increased subscriptions
- What it could mean for individual team members
  * Learn new skills
  * Lead the team in a new direction

There may not be a discussion of next steps since Bruce and his direct reports are responsible for them. If he had a next step that was consistent across the organization, this would be the place to add it. Next steps might be different for different teams or individuals. The presenter shouldn't go into that level of detail while everyone is present. His wrap up might be more of an inspiration ask that all employees get behind the new direction and the new leaders.

Scenario #3: CUSTOMERS & PRODUCTS IMPACT

Chandler is excited to get to the Impact in his storyline because he wants to prove out his promise:
By implementing our two-minute tool, you can increase loans by 50%.

In this presentation, the Solution element went through case studies and implementation options, timetable, and costs. And while the case studies may have presented interesting results, implementing a new Solution is never without its challenges. Nothing happens tomorrow without somebody modifying the way things are done today. So, while interested, Chandler's prospects also anticipate the work ahead. Chandler wants the Impact element of his talk track to motivate prospects to embrace the necessary changes in order to get the desired outcome.

He would do well to go back to his case studies and show the real results of each program, potentially expanding to discuss the broader reach of results and statistics that back up the success of LoanLogic. He might also introduce some best practices used by other organizations. The emphasis on positive results sways the prospects in the direction of outcome to be gained and away from the cost or challenge of getting there.

Here are the talking points:

- Best practices to increase loan interest and applications

- Getting to 50% completion rate

- Next step: pilot in financial institution

Chandler's next step might be to propose a pilot in the financial institution or to take a deeper look at the institution's current loan process to discern where his solution best fits. He should have a first step or easy step in mind to keep the conversation with the customer moving forward.

The first and third scenarios have specific Next Steps and the second scenario has a more personal and inspirational one. The Next Step talking point is the easiest to add to the Impact element and is often forgotten. One communicator described this as follows: "I'm good at getting them to 'So what?' but I always seem to forget to answer the 'Now what?'" That's true of a lot of presentations. A communicator will have more success if he assumes the best possible outcome from his storyline. They're with him, they agree, so now what? The talk track wraps up with the first step they can take to move forward.

As you review our methodology and the concept behind each of the elements, keep in mind that this is a model, not a mandate. Our intent is to help people organize storylines that move listeners to a clear destination. Our tools have proven themselves across thousands of presentations.

But they are just that: tools. The best communicators take the tools, understand the methodology, and then modify according to their circumstances.

Sometimes, it means moving the Implementation map from the Solution element to the Impact/Next Step element. That's fine. Depending on the topic, an implementation plan can be a discussion point of a proposed Solution or just the Next step to move forward.

Sometimes it means going back and adjusting the overall message to better fit the storyline. That's fine too, as long as it has a clear and measurable value to the listener.

Sometimes, it means leaving out a lot of great points because they just don't fit the structure. That's more than fine; in fact, it's a critical checkpoint for any communicator because it means that clarity for the listener has taken priority over everything the presenter wanted to say.

Developing a storyline isn't easy, but it works. It's the simplicity of the elements that brings clarity to the details. The next chapter pulls all the storyline elements together to illustrate the flow of communication in each of the three presentations.

11

Storylines for Three Scenarios

In the last four chapters, we've developed each element of
the storyline separately. Most of the discussion centered
on what the communicator needs to accomplish. But since
communication begins with the listener's perspective, it is
important to review the flow of each presentation to see if
the listeners' expectations are met.

There are three questions that should guide a presenter
through their outlines. If I were the listener, would I...

- Understand what the communicator wants to
  accomplish?

- Understand how the communicator plans to take
  me through the topic?

- Hear the proof points needed to buy into the idea?

Here are the full storylines for the scenarios.

DATA SECURITY - PRESENTATION

Susan needs to raise concern about increased risks without an enterprise protocol. Her recommendation is to stall the project for 60 days while she gets a new protocol in place.

Here's her outline:

| MESSAGE | If we delay the analytics product launch for 60 days, we can adopt security protocols to eliminate up to 20% added risks of a data breach. |

OVERVIEW OF FRAMEWORK

Today, I want to talk about:
- The shift in protocol with our adoption of smart technologies (Situation)
- Options for building an enterprise solution (Solution)
- Risk expectation and reduction within 60 days (Impact/Next Steps)

SITUATION

EXTERNAL PERSPECTIVE

- Consumers want products to share information and offer one consistent response.
- Smart technologies require products and solutions to share all they know.
- Companies have to build interfaces that allow their solutions to exchange information.
- Open architectures are up to 20% more vulnerable to data breaches.

INTERNAL PERSPECTIVE

- Our products were built on closed architectures, and we don't share data across divisions.
- We have minimal security threats because of strong firewalls uniquely built for each division.

SPECIFIC PROGRAM OR INITIATIVES

- SmartLine is our smart technology that will leverage data across seven divisions.
- To build SmartLine, we removed the firewalls that protect data in each division.
- This increases access points for breaches and puts us at a 20% higher risk of exposure.

WHAT I'M SOLVING FOR

- Can we develop an enterprise security protocol quickly to protect data from all divisions?

SOLUTION

- Three Options for Enterprise Security Strategies
- Best Practices from Security Vendors
- Vendor Recommendation
- Implementation Plan
- Development Impact and Timing Options
- 60 Day Plan

IMPACT/ NEXT STEPS

- Costs of Exposure – Magnitude of a breach to the enterprise
- Costs of 60 Day Delay
- Next Step: Buy-in with Development Teams
- Next Step: Hire vendor

So, what are the takeaways? It's clear that Susan believes the risk is high enough to delay the development team while she puts a new protocol in place. In fact, she has estimated the increased risk factor and has examples to back up her recommendation. She explains why the system-wide protocol hasn't been there to date and aligns the challenge with the decisions of other companies so that her leaders will know that the increased risks are not unique to their organization.

Susan's listeners won't like the delay, but she sets up the discussion to help them make an informed decision. I would expect the listeners to focus on the costs associated with the decision they make. They'll care less about who would help her build the protocol and how she found vendors.

Bruce is trying to get a new sports package into the market so that he can increase subscriptions. He has six months to take a competitive lead, so he's bringing in new resources to get a package to market quickly.

Here's his outline:

MESSAGE

By adding capabilities outside of our experience, we can launch a sports package that could double our subscriptions in 6 months.

OVERVIEW OF FRAMEWORK

Today, I want to talk about:
- Challenges with sports loyalty and subscriptions (Situation)
- Our Strategy to change our game and what we need to do it (Solution)
- And what it means for us, collectively and individually. (Impact/Next Steps)

SITUATION

EXTERNAL PERSPECTIVE

- Sports programming drives three times the viewers of any other programming.
- Competition is fierce, as all content providers want to capture the sports enthusiast wallet.
- Subscriptions are the best way to maximize sales, but viewers aren't interested in the packages.
- Sports viewers like most activities linked to pregame and post-game shows and events.
- Research shows that viewers also participate in sports chat rooms and fantasy leagues.

INTERNAL PERSPECTIVE

- For the past three years, our subscriptions have produced minimal results.
- Viewing dropped off during subscription life, so value wasn't delivered as advertised.
- Sports enthusiasts haven't stopped viewing; but they shifted preferences based on hype and offerings.

SPECIFIC PROGRAM OR INITIATIVES

- Our team has an interactive concept that could capture and retain viewers.
- It requires gaming sophistication to allow for sequencing and real-time interaction.
- We don't' have this expertise on our team today.

WHAT I'M SOLVING FOR

- Can we add resources to accelerate this concept and bring it to the marketplace in six months?

SOLUTION

- Capabilities we need and how to get them
- Profiles of leaders who are joining the team
- How we will leverage their skills in six months
- What will shift in organization and responsibilities
- Big goals for six month plan

IMPACT/ NEXT STEPS

- What it could mean for our business
  - Innovation leader
  - Increased subscriptions
- What it could mean for you
  - Learn new skills
  - Lead us in a new direction

What is the listeners' perspective? I suspect they will be torn between the excitement of working on a new and innovative product and uncertainty about the changes necessary to make that project successful. Bruce does a good job of setting up the changes as opportunity and explaining how the product concept came to be. As a listener, you can follow his thinking and you feel excited about the possibility he puts forth. His team might be surprised by how he plans to solve for the gap, but if he communicates clearly, they will also understand the value of the capabilities that he's bringing in and the new leaders will sound like resources instead of threats.

Most employees will leave the meeting a little worried about their specific managers but curious about their own opportunities and excited about the new energy and direction the leader is taking. Because the managers impacted have already heard this news and support the new organization structure, any remaining concerns among the employees can be minimized in follow-up meetings led by the managers.

CUSTOMERS & PRODUCTS - PRESENTATION

Chandler is eager to get the new product into financial institutions. He wants to position his product as an innovative way to improve the loan application process and significantly impact the number of approved loans.

Here's his outline:

MESSAGE

By implementing our two-minute tool, you can increase loans by 50%.

OVERVIEW OF FRAMEWORK

Today, I want to talk about:
- The Impact of personal behaviors on choices
- Our algorithms for linking personal and financial data
- And the impact on your loan process

SITUATION

EXTERNAL PERSPECTIVE

- Consumer behaviors and habits say a lot about what they value and how they spend money.
- Social media holds a lot of data about activities and can predict spending patterns.
- Studies prove that aligning with someone's behavior on social media can lift sales by 40%.

INTERNAL PERSPECTIVE

- Financial firms look at what people earn and don't have data on what people do.
- Loans are driven more by what I would like to do than what I actually do.
- Most on-line applications take five minutes to complete and 48 hours for reply.
- Financial institutions experience 45% incomplete rate on loan applications.

SPECIFIC PROGRAM OR INITIATIVES

- Mall kiosk test positioned financing next to something people would like to own.
- Voice-activation technology drove a conversation about behaviors and choices.
- Algorithm linked interview responses with financial data for insights and assumptions.
- Kiosks drove high participation, increased leads, higher qualification rates and increased sales

WHAT I'M SOLVING FOR

- Can we help you increase loan applications and your loan closure rate?

SOLUTION

- The science of the LoanLogic algorithm
- Case studies of financial institutions
- Integration options: website vs. free-standing kiosks
- Timetable and expected costs

IMPACT/ NEXT STEPS

- Best practices to increase loan interest and applications
- Getting to 50% completion rate
- Next step: Pilot in financial institution

What's the listener's perspective? Innovation and analytics jump out in this conversation. This young company seems to have an intriguing way to capture insights that most financial institutions don't have. The listener will take note of the fact that the salesperson seems to know his industry and the challenges associated with approving loans. Loans generate revenue for the bank, and they'd like to capture and convert more of these opportunities.

I think in this case the listener will be sold on the success of the algorithm but also wondering about the ease of integrating the product. It's good that there are options to consider and the offer of a pilot could push the listener to action. This is likely a decision that spans multiple departments within a bank, so the listener will have to be willing to share the discussion and get others on board. The communicator has given him good sound bites in the Situation to help carry the idea forward.

Each of the scenarios illustrates how a journey has been laid out for the listener. The ideal presentation flow is also referenced as a resource at the end of this book.

Here's the bottom line: a strong storyline ensures that the listener is willing to participate in the journey. That's the point of communication: to bring clarity to ideas so that a listener can engage in a topic and consider the outcome that you believe is possible.

Once that storyline is set, the visuals and supporting materials become much easier to produce.

12

From Storylines to Visuals

The most important point I can make about visuals is that they should be compiled after the development of the outline. But, communicators don't always build content that way. Instead, they begin with the visuals and use the structure of the visuals to guide the structure of the talk track.

Unintentionally, that makes the talk track a linear conversation. It means that the communicator is building a storyline from the bottom-up through a series of specific points rather than from the top down, connecting big ideas and aligning points under those ideas. The bottom-up approach is linear because there aren't the pivot points in the flow of ideas to help the listener understand the overall direction.

When visuals are the foundation of the talk track, listeners hear one point after another, and it can feel like a communicator is simply running down a list of data points. From the discussion of the listener's perspective in Chapter 2, this approach misses many of the listener's needs: the point of the presentation, the direction of the talk track, and how the speaker plans to lead them through it.

When visuals and supporting materials are developed to support the outline, the communicator owns the talk track instead of relying on slideware and does a better job of showcasing the intention behind the visuals.

As we work across organizations, we see visuals as a common method of sharing storylines. And we see the frustration that presenters go through when they're asked to change their presentation or to present something that someone else organized. We do an exercise in our workshop to illustrate the difference in complexity when someone is asked to present ideas following someone else's details rather than someone else's intent. We begin with a series of points and allow two different presenters to see how they organize information differently. It isn't vastly different, but it's different enough to throw the presenters off course because the order of ideas doesn't resonate with them.

Then we introduce our framework and allow the presenters to work together to organize points into the three elements: Situation, Solution, Impact/Next Step. They realize that they readily agree on placement of the points under the three elements, and then they can adjust the points under each element to suit their own approach to the talk track.

This illustrates the value of the framework which helps another presenter or anyone on a support team see the overarching goal of the storyline. When we complete the exercise above, the takeaway is always: "We didn't take all the same steps, but we ended up on the same path and reached the same outcome." That's the benefit of understanding the journey.

When communicators don't have consensus around the storyline, the input they get is frustrating, and it often impacts their openness to feedback or success with the presentation.

You may have heard a presenter say, "I'm not sure what Melissa meant on this slide. But I'll talk you through my interpretation."

That means the order of someone's points don't make sense to another presenter, but she feels restricted in how she goes through the material.

Or perhaps you've heard:

> "This is an eye chart. You don't need to look at the details on the slide. I just wanted to make one point."

That means someone had a visual already created and is trying to force it onto an idea. It isn't really the point they want to make, but it's what they have.

The most common complaint I hear is:

> "I'm not sure where this is going anymore. So many people have added to this deck that it's become fragmented to me and it's now my boss's voice instead of mine."

This happens because the boss is editing slides instead of reviewing the storyline. When we don't know where information is headed, we assume the communicator doesn't either. So, we add information to "help them out." Only it isn't helpful; it weighs a presentation down and adds distracting tangents.

So, outline first!

Support materials have evolved a lot, and it's just as common to see a communicator with no visuals as someone who uses PPT or Prezi. Videos have become a great way to elicit emotion.

Communicators should keep a few guiding principles in mind.

The visual is a guide for the listener, not the communicator. Knowing how the listener responds to the structure of a slide will help presenters prioritize visual choices.

Listeners respond to shape first, color second, and words last.

Listeners recognize the relationship between shapes on a page or slide first. In fact, the point of using a visual is usually to illustrate a relationship. Is something growing bigger, moving faster, or showing a different pattern than something else? Is one thing a portion of something else? The guiding principle is to ensure that the shapes on the page represent the alignment that the presenter is trying to create. Shapes that repeat help listeners trace a concept through the presentation and remember it afterwards.

Colors are the second recognition factor.

People respond to color and look for what they think the color is saying. The eye is naturally drawn to brighter colors, so it's easiest to show a change or difference by contrasting a bright color to a darker one.

There are some colors that have universal meaning, and it's important to use them correctly, particularly on charts and graphs. Red is consistently used to represent something negative, something stopping, "being in the red," etc., and green represents something positive or something that is moving forward. Colors don't have to be universal to send signals, though. Using colors consistently in the same deck will send a clear enough message. If blue represents programs that are top priorities on one slide, it can't represent the programs that we are sunsetting on the next slide.

Most companies create a color palette for presentation materials. Be sure that you use colors consistently. When a color is used with consistent meaning throughout a deck, it can be a very effective way to help listeners follow complex ideas.

The last recognition factor is words. Listeners prefer pictures over text. It's a bit of a contradiction in spoken communication to ask listeners to read, isn't it?

Presenters use a lot of slides that have just words or bullets on them. This conflicts with the value of a visual which is to help a listener understand the relationship between multiple points. And, a list of bullets don't have a relationship to a listener; they usually represent a level of detail or a laundry list of points. So, the communicator has to work hard to link these thoughts to each other.

Use these guidelines to improve delivery. Avoid a series of bullet slides and keep each slide to no more than five points; this prevents the presenter from overdoing the details. Avoid complete sentences on the bullet slides; start with action verbs instead. This helps the presenter punch key concepts before elaborating.

13

The Keynote Exception

To wrap up the discussion of storylines, I want to call out one exception to the flow of ideas: the keynote address. Our team works on a lot of keynotes each year, from all-hands meetings to client conferences and leadership summits, all designed to paint vision and direction for where companies are headed.

As listeners, we usually think of keynotes as the storylines of the top leaders because they communicate the direction of a company or set the themes of industry events. But they aren't the only communicators who set vision, as I called out in the opening of the book. If communicators lead a big department, they set the goals and big initiatives for the department. If communicators manage a project team, they set the picture of what they're trying to accomplish or the three-year journey to get to a new operating model.

When vision and direction are the most important elements to set in a storyline, there can be an alternative way to build it.

All of the concepts presented in Chapters 5–10 still apply, but the order may be adjusted to create a more compelling journey for the listener.

The communication in Scenario #2 is the most likely to have been a keynote before it was an update meeting. I set up the scenario as a leader who had determined that he needed additional resources and skills to help his team move to a new sports concept and package. We laid out the flow of the storyline to identify why a new approach to subscriptions was needed, his team's idea to build a new, interactive package and what it will take to get the package to market.

The full outline in Chapter 11 shows how he will lead his team from understanding the opportunity to uncovering challenges they will have and how he is going to help them move forward.

Imagine that he delivered a keynote to his peer group a year prior to this meeting in order to position the possibility of a new way of thinking about subscriptions. The storyline in the previous chapters puts them close to an implementation plan. But his interest in this idea would have started some time ago. At that time, he might have delivered a keynote to inspire his peers and leaders to think differently and look for innovation and ideas outside of their industry. He wouldn't have known the answer at the time, much less been ready to think about bringing in outside resources.

We would have shifted the storyline elements to help him start with a forward look or future vision. The elements shift around like this:

Current State:

Message ----Situation ----Solution-----Impact/Next Step

Future State:

Message ------ Impact ------- Situation -------- Solution

The message is still a critical piece to the storyline, but it's less about an ask and more about a vision. The presenter may not even have an ask at this point. In a keynote, the message is often used more as a tagline and an inspiration. It's less measurable and more about possibility. The message of a keynote can become the theme of the year or the theme of a conference.

In Scenario #2, the division leader's message might be:

- Our next step is a quantum leap.

- Focus on what people do, not what they ask for.

- Let's win the pennant instead of the game.

His goal is to inspire his company to think very differently and well outside their current roadmap to find a way to attract viewers to a subscription model.

In the framework phase, he moves the Impact to the front of the storyline and focuses on a future state. The goal is not about measurement but about possibility.

IMPACT/FUTURE STATE

- Imagine…an experience that lasts through a full season.

- Imagine…a virtual place where sports fans can interact, participate, and debrief on every game.

- It will happen. It is already happening in different places and in different ways.

- Who has the capability? What are they doing? How can we re-create it?

- Connecting the experience is a transformational opportunity.

- Our vision for the sports fans experience.

- The future state paints a picture of what could happen and builds a level of excitement and possibility.

Then the speaker leads the audience to the Situation points. The Situation remains the company's current state.

SITUATION

External:

- Competition is fierce for subscriptions and everyone wants to capture the sports enthusiast's wallet.

- Viewers aren't interested in existing packages because they don't enhance the experience.

- Sports enthusiasts create their own experiences using lots of different resources.

- **Internal:**

- Our recent focus groups suggested focusing on what people do rather than what they ask for.

- We have mapped the "ideal experience" based on sports enthusiasts' actions and interests.

- There are over 30 different elements of sports experience from fantasy leagues to interactive games and chat rooms with players.

Specific:

- Today, each viewer's experience is unique and multifaceted.

- No one knows how to weave it together.

- It would require a holistic experience that tracked from a sports season's beginning to end.

Solve for?

- Could we build an interactive concept that delivers the ultimate viewer experience?

The funneling concept is relevant here. The bullets above follow the methodology, but the talk track is focused on leading the listeners to a possibility. It's less about what we don't have as a company and more about a gap in the industry. The division leader has shifted from future state as a forward-looking possibility to current state and why the industry hasn't explored this.

The Situation still sets up the pivot to the Solution. The speaker isn't addressing specific challenges at this time, but creating interest in how his team could explore this.

SOLUTION

- Let's explore the possibilities.

- We'll need to think outside the box to define the ultimate experience.

- Blueprint the "cutting edge" solution.

- What it should be will get us to what it could be.

NEXT STEPS

- What should we do differently?
- Think outside the box
- Focus on what to do instead of how to do it
- Let the customer lead the way

The speaker knows that the leaders and his peers won't walk out with action steps. That's not what he's going for. Instead, he wants the leaders to put themselves in the position of the consumer and reimagine the ultimate experience. He wants to create energy and excitement about the vision, and he wants his peer group to feel a part of it.

Some keynotes address large employee groups where the communicator will go from an industry perspective to a personal takeaway in less than 30 minutes. These keynotes move listeners through a storyline that starts with a broad vision and ends with a specific task or belief for every individual in the room.

But even when the order of the storyline shifts, the keynote communicators want to have the same impact on listeners as every communicator does. And it's this: listeners reach the destination of the storyline and they have memorable elements of the storyline that they will repeat to others. Communicators want ideas to be repeated to build support and momentum across an organization

Storylines need stories to help ideas take hold. And that's when great communicators focus on how to connect stories into a storyline.

The Pivot Point

From Science to Art

You've hit the midpoint of the book, and you have a decision to make.

You've walked through the fundamentals of storylines—the flow of ideas that lead the listener to a clear and measurable outcome. This is the science of communication. It's a lot to learn, but it is learnable. I've coached thousands of people on adapting and implementing the tools that you read about in the first two sections.

Across your career, you may build storylines or you may have others help you pull the storyline together. It's the best way to organize content, and it will lead the listener to where you want them to go.

But the decision you need to make is: Is structure enough?

If you can communicate in a way that leads your listeners to the desired outcome, will you be effective enough as a communicator? Many would say yes. If that's you, then our work is complete. You have the science and several examples of how to execute it.

But if you're reading this book because you believe in the power of communication to move people and you want to be the compelling storyteller that you met in the opening chapter, then your journey continues.

The pivot point comes as we move from the science of communication to the art. Developing this art is more of a marathon than a sprint. Mastering communication is a career-long journey, and what you really hope to master is consistency.

Communication is one of the few durable skills a person will carry throughout their career and across different jobs. From the day you start your career, it is a skill that can set you apart. And until the day you retire, it will be a skill that defines how your colleagues relate to you. You'll be hired for it and evaluated based on it. You'll be praised when it works and critiqued when it doesn't. The challenges you face will often trace back to breakdowns in communication.

Becoming an effective communicator isn't a "check the box" kind of skill. It's acquired by ongoing assessment and evolving expectations.

Remember from the first chapter that many communicators avoid telling stories because they think it's an advanced communication skill or because they think it isn't worth the risk if the story flops.

Yet communication is all about taking risks. It is the most vulnerable and electrifying skill that you can develop. It's the skill that no one will develop for you, no one will deliver for you...and no one tells you how challenging it can be until you try to master it. The high expectations people have for communicators may become apparent to you the first time you speak before a large audience, deliver a keynote, or lead a customer conference. Those expectations can feel like the weight of the world on your shoulders—because the success of the event and the takeaways of the conference are riding on your ability to set them up well. It all comes down to your communication skills.

That's a powerful feeling ---- and a very intimidating one. It is all about the ability to connect. And, it isn't acquired overnight. This is the marathon, not the sprint.

So, we pivot at this point in the book and move to the harder elements for the communicator:

The mastery of storytelling!

Section 3

The Art of Stories

14

Telling Great Stories

Listeners like stories in a business context because it helps them remember and repeat ideas. But when we asked people we surveyed about stories, they told us that they don't hear stories often and, when they do, they don't repeat them because the stories aren't relevant or don't align with the topic. They thought stories would be more memorable if they were more relatable and if the presenter was a better storyteller.

In order to solve for those expectations, we formed focus groups to watch and listen to people telling stories. Our goal was to observe how people tell stories so that we could identify commonalities and develop best practices. But what we found communicators had in common were the mistakes they make, not what they do well. The takeaways from these sessions validated a lot of what people had told us in our third-party survey.

- "The stories themselves aren't always interesting."
- "Many storytellers aren't great at delivery."
- "Listeners get frustrated trying to figure out the point of a disjointed or rambling narrative."

In short, our most consistent takeaway was that many people find it hard to tell a story well.

We also asked focus group participants about stories they hear in business settings. Here's what they said:

- "We tell stories about our brand; not about our people."

- "Stories that I hear and repeat hit me emotionally, not logically."

- "We talk about stories, but we don't use them."

- "One in a hundred stories that I hear are worth repeating. But when I hear a good one, I use it over and over again."

In the focus groups, we also tested whether participants could remember and retell a story.

One participant used a personal story to illustrate to a group of new hires that they were joining a great company. Here's Craig's story:

> Five years ago, I'd been out of work for almost a year. My search for an IT management job took longer than I thought, and it was stressful on me and on my family. We were so grateful when I was offered a job here, and I started working in early November. I didn't have my confidence back yet, so I was concerned when I was called into my manager's office after just three weeks. Unbeknownst to me, each department here has a tradition of giving away a holiday turkey, and my manager had selected me. He seemed to know that my family had been going through a tough time, and it was a wonderful gift. That's when I knew this is a company that cares about its people. You've made the right decision to work here.

The participants' feedback? They wanted more emotion. They wanted to feel a personal connection to Craig's stress level before landing a job.

Here's how I retold the story:

I know as you sit here, you are a little unsure of what it will be like to work here. I can tell you that in short order, you'll realize that you haven't just accepted a job, you've joined a family.

That's certainly how I felt five years ago. I was an IT manager who'd been let go from another company during downsizing. I had a solid skill set and thought it would be pretty easy to find another position. I was wrong. I was out of work for almost a year. If any of you have been through this, you know how hard it is being out of work that long. I'd passed the point of stressed out. I was beginning to genuinely worry about how I'd take care of my family.

It was a huge relief to be offered a role here and to get started in early November. Things were still a little stressful; we'd fallen behind on some bills and I was still playing catch up. But we had a way forward and I hoped the situation would improve by the new year. I didn't talk about this with my new coworkers, but I always carried that weight with me. Three weeks later when I was summoned to my manager's office, I could feel my stress neurons firing. Surely I hadn't messed up already. What could he want?

Well. Unbeknownst to me at that time, the company's tradition is to give away a turkey to someone in every department, and my manager thought it might make

> a difference for me that year. Boy, was he right! We
> were living week to week. Thanksgiving wasn't even on
> my radar. That simple act of kindness was a big gesture
> to my family. The fact that my manager had noticed
> something was off and wanted to support me—that
> was a powerful signal to me that this company is an
> extended family. So the message I want you to hear
> today is: welcome to the family!

I asked the group again after my version and found that the group remembered the emotion in the story and connected with it more.

We continued the exercise of listening to stories and then I repeated each story. Each time we asked for observations based on the storyteller's version and mine. Here are some of the groups' observations:

- The story took longer when I told it, but it didn't feel long.

- The people and circumstances were more relatable.

- My story seemed to include the listeners.

- My version of the story expressed more emotion.

As we worked with each group to rework their stories, we found three key elements that many of their stories were missing:

A Point: Many of the initial stories told in the focus groups left participants thinking, "So what? Why did you just tell me about that?" This matched what we learned from our survey participants as well. Listeners often feel that most stories don't have a point or any direction at all. This is something most people have experienced at some point. Speakers fail to tell a story well because they get too bogged down in details or they add elements to a story that really aren't relevant to the takeaway.

When we asked the focus group participants about the flow of their stories, we found that many of them were simply relating the events as the details came back to them. They had little structure in mind. That lack of structure is precisely what leads to rambling and disjointedness.

Listener Interest: Some of the stories did have a point, but either they were boring or the storyteller failed to make the audience feel like a part of the experience.

We then worked to retell the stories with more texture, more detail. Listeners in the focus groups confirmed that the details made a significant difference in what they remembered.

The storytellers were surprised at this. In my retellings, the added context came from questions we asked the storytellers after they had initially told their stories. It wasn't new information; they just hadn't included that level of detail in their stories because they didn't perceive the need for it. This ties back to the risk associated with telling stories. Most speakers don't know how much detail is too much or too little, or what kinds of details make a story interesting. When I retold some of the stories, I added texture by focusing on things we wanted the listener to relate to in the story.

It was another important proof point that stories can take a while to tell. Several of our storytellers were worried about this. They weren't giving themselves permission to embellish the story enough to make it interesting.

Listener Response: Few stories actually drew a response from the listeners. While people were willing to listen, they didn't have comments or questions afterward, unless to ask for clarification or because they had missed the point. The listeners didn't give reactions, share similar experiences or seem impacted by the stories.

Our observation was that storytellers were simply sharing experiences and not working to make the experience matter to the listeners. If stories are told well, they are the elements of a presentation that will be remembered and repeated, because listeners relate to them. But the stories told in our focus groups weren't accomplishing this.

In response to what we learned from these focus groups, we now had insights on common gaps in storytelling. But, we still wanted to capture best practices and see if there were commonalities in people who tell stories well.

So, we continued our research by asking companies to introduce us to their best storytellers. And the most common response we got was a blank stare. This seemed to have something to do with the aura that people attach to great storytellers and the lack of compelling communicators in company cultures. The term "storyteller" is loaded. People expect a master communicator, an entertainer. So we changed our question. We began asking for the people who bring ideas to life and who seem to put context around their thoughts. We compiled a list of storytellers from a number of companies and interviewed them to test the mechanics of storytelling we'd hypothesized.

Our earlier research had shown that people who tell stories find it easy. This new round of interviews reaffirmed this. Many of the storytellers we interviewed had been telling stories for so long that their approach was more habitual than intentional. We had to dissect their habits to get at the principles that made their storytelling effective.

So with the challenges identified in focus groups and the habits we observed in good storytellers, we were able to identify three principles that are universal to good storytellers.

And, it's these three principles that we help every aspiring storyteller learn how to do.

Build **Structure** + Add **Interest** + Transfer **Emotion**

Build Structure: Every effective storyteller we interviewed has a clear sense of direction. They know where the story begins, how it ends, and where the "aha" moment should occur for the listener.

Because they are effective communicators, most people assume the flow happens by chance. But, it isn't so. Every storyteller we interviewed has a structure behind their story.

This explains the less effective storytellers we studied in the focus groups. They're trying to imitate something without understanding it. Those who don't have a clear sense of structure and direction end up telling a haphazard story. Those who plan the story's structure and practice it give a smooth presentation that feels unrehearsed...but virtually never is.

The great storytellers are very purposeful in how they organize the story. They have thought through the flow of the story as much as the flow of the storylines. They know their stories, and they practice them before sharing them.

Add Interest: The great storytellers add color commentary to their stories. They know that details bring the story to life, making it memorable and worth repeating.

Again, the gap between great storytellers who do this well and the ones I saw struggle in our focus groups was more about intention. The good storytellers wanted the story to be interesting and relatable to the listeners and so they added "color" throughout it to have multiple places where the audience can connect to the story.

Transfer Emotion: As I listened to hundreds of stories over the course of our research, I was fascinated by why people respond to some stories and don't respond to others. What was the magic that made some stories work and others flop? It's emotion. Great storytellers don't just want you to hear their stories. They want you to feel them.

I observed that great storytellers keep working for a response from listeners as they tell a story. I know that's true in how I tell a story. I'm willing to take the time and the risk to see if I can elicit an emotional response to a story, and when I asked the great storytellers about this, they all agreed. They know how they want their audience to feel, and they are engaged enough with listeners that they can read that reaction throughout the story.

These three concepts seem to set good storytellers apart. The structure is the science of stories, but it leads to the art of creating interest and transferring emotion. It's a tough formula, and it takes a while to master it. I think that's why many people don't work at it.

But that's a missed opportunity in leveraging the power of communication. I don't think the divide of communication should come down to those who can tell stories and those who can't. Companies need good storytellers to ensure that ideas spread across companies.

The next three chapters will describe the tools we use to help communicators develop skills around each of these three principles.

15

The Structure of Stories

Much like a storyline, a story has to have a structure that leads the listener to a point. It can take twists and turns along the way, and in fact, that's what makes it interesting. But understanding the difference between a wild turn and a little bend in the journey is difficult for most communicators. Structure ensures that the narrative stays on track.

Here's a scenario to illustrate how stories take wild turns.

You're listening to a talk about forgiveness. The speaker sets the stage by telling you that an important attribute in friendship is forgiveness. It reminds him of a story about his childhood friend, Randy:

When I was eight, I used to go fishing every Friday afternoon with my friend, Randy. There was a fishing hole about a mile from our neighborhood, and we would grab our poles after school and walk down there. Funny thing about our neighborhood was that there were a lot of young guys our age, but Randy and I were the only two who liked to fish. We lived on a street named Trout Way, so it seemed like there should have been more aspiring fishermen, right?

Anyway, Randy and I went fishing on Fridays after school, and we would stop at the small grocery to get a soda and snack on the way. That little store had been there for about a hundred years. I can still see Ms. Rose standing behind the counter. She wore her hair up in a big bun, and we used to guess how long it must be. Eventually, that little store became an important inheritance. The real estate was a prime location for the interstate they added ten years later, and Ms. Rose's family sold it to the state for a handsome fee. Today, her descendants are the largest landowners in that portion of the state.

Anyway, one Friday, Randy was talking too much during our fishing trip, and he wasn't paying attention to his line. He got a bite, and the fish yanked the pole right out of his hand and twisted his line into mine creating a tangled mess. We couldn't get the lines apart, Randy's fish pulled hard, and my pole snapped. I'd gotten my pole from my uncle, and it was a nice one. I was not happy.

Randy was mad he lost the fish, but I was furious that I lost my best fishing pole. I didn't speak to him for a week. And after a week, my father asked me why I wasn't fishing with Randy. I said I hated Randy. My father said I needed to learn to forgive. He talked to me about the importance of friendship and not letting anger or frustration get in the way of friends. It was my first lesson about forgiveness.

As you can see, the story meanders, even taking a wild detour into the small store and the land barons of the county. It's too disjointed. The listener can't stay connected to the central narrative.

When communicators don't have a plan for the flow of the story, they wander off into memories and side points that were a part of their experience, but not at all relevant to the direction of the story. It's important to organize a story that carries the listeners along.

As I built a formula for a clear and compelling structure, more than one type of story emerged: the Experience Story and the Data Story.

Experience Stories are more common. They are based on personal experience, and they're designed to draw the listener into a moment in time or a situation that relates to the broader topic. These stories are often well received and are highly adaptable—the story can be tailored so that it is relevant to any group.

We designed five steps to help a communicator structure an Experience Story:

1. **Set the Stage:** Give the listener some context for the story. What is it about, when and where did it happen, and who are the key players?

2. **Introduce Conflict:** All good stories have conflict or a point at which something has to be resolved. It could be an opportunity instead of a problem. A story needs a reason for something to change, something to be improved or something to be solved.

3. **Solve the Problem:** Once there's an issue or opportunity, the story will logically move toward a solution.

4. **End with Impact:** This is the result of resolving the problem or seizing the opportunity. The impact needs to be significant enough—good or bad—for listeners to feel it was worth their time to get involved in the story.

5. **Wrap it Up:** At the end, the story must connect back to the storyline.

As we've worked with people on this methodology, we find they tend to struggle with the first two steps. They're tempted to shortchange on context, but context is precisely where the listener takes an interest. Characters come to life, a setting is familiar or interesting, or new information is revealed about the communicator. Good storytellers set the stage to get listeners interested from the moment the story begins.

The point of conflict is a pivot for the listener. They will either relate to the story at this point or they will disengage because it doesn't seem relevant to them. Many communicators seem to simply tell the conflict rather than illustrating it in a story because they believe the solution is the most interesting part.

That's a disconnect. The listener's connection with someone else's story comes more from empathizing with a challenge or believing in an opportunity. Listeners have to believe either situation is real before they'll take an interest in the solution.

Data Stories explain complex points or heaps of data. These stories are based on facts and insights derived from those facts that haven't been proven out yet. They don't have as much room for embellishment as the experience story, but they are useful in helping listeners understand the potential impact of otherwise dry information. And, they are an effective way to help someone process data and consider what the data may actually mean.

The data story is used when insights are gathered, but no conclusion or specific actions around the insights has occurred. The story is still active, in other words; it isn't resolved or completed yet. Data stories are more about questions than answers. So, the structure of the story is modified to set up a hypothesis instead of a challenge. Then, rather than ending with impact, it positions options or recommendations.

We designed five steps to help a communicator structure a data story.

1. **Set the Stage:** This gives listeners context for the topic, provides background and anticipates any questions the audience might have about the data.

2. **Introduce Insights:** Share your insights and observations behind the data.

3. **Hypothesis from Insights:** This is where the presenter discusses the most viable conclusions drawn from the data and insights so far.

4. **Options/Recommendations:** Rather than discussing the impact, this phase presents the steps the presenter thinks the group should consider based on the insights and hypothesis.

5. **Wrap up:** Complete the story by referring back to the initial question and stating what you plan to do to follow-up on your recommendation.

Imagine that you're part of a sales team that rolled out a new product. There's a lot of expectation around the product, and you've been given training, sales tools, and marketing materials to position it with your customer base. But customer response has been minimal. Customers don't seem as interested as your marketing team predicted they would be, and your team's numbers are suffering because of it. Most of the sales teams have been complaining about it and are hoping that the product will be revamped or the quotas will be shifted. You're headed into the quarterly sales meeting to see what your manager has to say about it.

This will be a tough meeting, and it's a common one across all companies. Things don't go as planned, groups hit roadblocks on initiatives, and leaders have to reset, realign, revise, and refocus their teams. There are likely to be at least two different leaders involved in this meeting: a sales leader and a marketing leader. I'll use the perspective of both leaders to illustrate two different kinds of stories.

SALES LEADER

Garrett knows his team is frustrated. He's frustrated, too. The marketing data continues to show that there is customer interest in the product, and upper management is putting pressure on him to get results. Garrett's observed a few meetings where he felt the salesperson didn't set the situation up well, and he caught himself doing the same thing recently. He knows the challenge is more with how the product is being positioned, rather than the product itself.

Garrett needs to open his team up to rethinking their sales strategy, and he'll share a story about his experience to illustrate a blind spot they may have.

Here's Garrett's story with the elements of the story divided into sections to illustrate the flow through each step.

EXPERIENCE STORY

Set the Stage

I know that you're frustrated with the lack of momentum around our new product, and I expect that you came to this meeting hoping to hear what I'm going to do about it. We have been digging deep into our projections and analytics, and we are going to share our findings with you.

I'm going to tell you right up front that they don't prove out what you're expecting them to. In fact, we're all going to be surprised by how strong the proof points are around this product. But before we talk any more about the product, I want to spend some time talking about us…and I want to call out a blind spot I think we may have. I know I have it.

It's the customer's perspective.

That might sound ridiculous... It might even anger you to even hear it. But I'm calling it out because I caught myself blind to the customer's perspective just a few weeks ago.

I've heard your frustration over the last few months, and I know it's real. I've been in many of the meetings with you, and I've also been disappointed with the lack of customer interest. So I decided to test the product myself, and I went back out into the field to position the demos and read customers' responses.

A few weeks ago, I took one of our newest sales engineers, Joe, with me. We were going to see Scott, a client and personal friend of mine, and I invited Joe to the meeting so that he could "see how it's done."

We went to the meeting, and I could tell Joe was impressed. Scott and I have a great relationship, and Scott talked openly about the successes and challenges of the last year. He even shared about a recent meeting with one of our competitors and told me that they are losing sales against our lead product at a ratio of 1:10. That was exciting insight! We had an easy conversation about our current products and some thoughts on what he may do in the year ahead. Then I told him I wanted him to see a new product, and I walked him through the demo.

I was surprised by his lack of questions, but I was confident in my presentation. I delivered the demo well, I knew my energy was invested in getting the features across, and Joe seemed to be taking it all in. Scott had another appointment waiting, so we wrapped up quickly and agreed to talk more about the product next time.

Introduce Conflict

Joe and I got in the car and as we drove away, I asked Joe for feedback on the meeting. I had an air of confidence because I knew it had gone well. It always does with Scott. But Joe hesitated and then said, "Well, I thought the demo missed the mark."

I wasn't sure what he meant. So, I asked again. Well, how do you think the meeting went? Joe said, "I thought the point of the meeting was to explore his potential need for our new product. I don't think we talked about that. I wasn't sure why he would be interested or what the product would solve for him. So, I didn't think showing him how it worked was very effective."

I was shocked….and embarrassed. As I listened to his comments, I realized Joe was right. I didn't involve Scott's perspective in the conversation at all. I was confident in our relationship, and I talked to him as if I knew what he needed. I never gave him a chance to actually say it. I was embarrassed that the newest salesperson called me on it……but he was right.

Solve the Problem

So here's what I did. I called Scott and asked for his feedback on the meeting. He didn't even remember the demo, but when questioned about it, he basically told me the same thing that Joe did. He was nice about it and joked with me. He said, "You know, you can take a leader out of sales, but you can't always take the sales out of a leader." That was Scott's way of telling me that I was talking and not listening. Bottom line: he hadn't focused on the product because he didn't think it was relevant for him.

End with Impact

Now, I'm not going to ask you to call your customers for feedback. But I am suggesting that you evaluate how you're positioning this. Are you the super salesperson like me—too focused on the excitement of the sale? Do you have a few Scotts in your accounts who have become so comfortable that they let you get away with talking about the product rather than their needs?

We have to listen to every account—no matter how well we know them—to continue to bring real value to their businesses.

That's why I think our first step in improving this product is improving ourselves.

Wrap Up

I'm going to focus my time this morning on bringing a fresh approach to positioning this product as a solution to customers' needs.

Garrett uses an experience story to show his own vulnerability and point out a blind spot in the sales approach. He'll be able to position a message about shifting their approach and engaging the group in the full storyline that introduces revised tools and best practices.

Assuming he is well regarded by his team, they'll be willing to consider their own shortcomings since Garrett was honest about his. He has created room in the discussion to admit what isn't working and to be open to finding new ways to sell this product. His portion of the meeting could then move to breakout groups or an open discussion about what others have experienced and what they think they can do to overcome it.

MARKETING LEADER

At some point during the meeting, the marketing leader, Mia, will also speak. She has the data and the facts that backup the opportunity for this product. Mia can present the facts as facts, or she can use a data story to position a hypothesis around what could be a missing element in the strategy for this product.

Here's how Mia might tell her story.

DATA STORY

Set the Stage

When we positioned the new product, we told you that we felt it would increase revenue by as much as 20% in your book of business. We were confident about that and worked hard to get you excited about it with a demo that highlights great features and a simple user experience.

Since we introduced the product four months ago, you've been frustrated and disappointed. I know because I've heard from many of you, and I've seen the minimal results in your sales numbers.

Introduce Insights

We revisited our initial data and assumptions about the product last month. We focused specifically on answering two things. First, were the projections accurate? They were. When surveyed about the value of this type of product, our customers and prospects say it is a definite need in their organizations. In fact, the needs assessment proved that interest is even higher than it was in our first survey three months ago. So the concept is right and the need is there.

Second, we checked to see if the interest is greater in one area of the company over another. And, that's where we gained additional insight. Initially, when we saw so much interest from our customers, we knew we had a home run. But when we went back through the data, we looked more closely to see who within our customer organizations had the highest response to the survey. And that's where we found an insight that we overlooked the first time.

Over 40% of the respondents came from customer marketing groups, instead of product groups. And while both groups expressed the same interest in features, they don't view the need for the product in the same way.

Hypothesis from Insights

Here's our hypothesis. We assumed you were talking to customer marketing groups as well as the product groups. And, you may be. But, we think you need to be talking to both groups together. We believe our customers' marketing groups can sell this product internally to their product groups and their need for the product will carry much more weight and urgency if they're a part of the same discussion.

Options/Recommendation

We need to build a storyline that brings marketing and product teams together to evaluate this product. We have reworked our positioning materials to support a conversation with both groups. We've tested it in five accounts this month, and we've received a great response.

The internal marketing groups told their product groups that our new product solves a significant pain point. A marketing group at one company told their colleagues that our product could improve efficiency in their reporting by as much as 40%!

It will be a more complex sell than we initially imagined because you will have to bring the marketing and product teams together. But it's worth it as we continue to capture data that proves the need and the revenue potential.

Wrap Up

We'd like to test the combined conversation in more of our accounts, and then come back to the group in 30 days with a revised sales strategy.

Let me explain more about the testing itself...

16

Creating Interest in Stories

Assume it's been a week since that quarterly sales meeting from the previous chapter occurred. We talked about the sales leader and the marketing leader, but there were many other things covered over the two-day meeting.

A week later, will you remember Garrett's and Mia's stories? Yes, but you may not know why you remember them.

This is because their stories had enough texture to them that there were a few sound bites that made the story stick.

From Garrett's story:

- Will you remember that Joe went with him on the sales call? Will you remember what Joe said about the demo missing the mark? How about your leader's reaction to the feedback?

- Will you remember Scott and the level of comfort that your leader has with him? Did you remember that they were personal friends? How about Scott's comment to Garrett: "You can't take the sales out of a leader?"

- You may even remember that Garrett was embarrassed and admitted it to you and that he went so far as to ask his friend for feedback.

Chances are good that if you respect Garrett, you'll think about your own approach. You may even change the way you're using the demo based on his story and the new ideas he shared later in his storyline. That's exactly the impact he wanted his story to have.

This story could have been told in three sentences.

CONDENSED VERSION

I want you to know that I tested the demo and invited a colleague to observe the sales call. He said it didn't go over well, so I called the customer and got similar feedback from the customer. I think we're missing the opportunity to align the product to the customer's needs.

The problem with this version is it has no life. For a story to have impact, the listeners should feel like they were there. Garrett's audience should relate to the feeling of his emotions dipping from confidence to total embarrassment, and to Joe's courage in giving honest feedback.

Depending on how well Garrett delivers it, his team will feel the tension in the story as he sets up the conflict. They weren't expecting Joe's feedback, and the sales leader should deliver the story in a way that shows his surprise as well.

I call these added elements the color commentary of a story. It's the added details that make a story memorable for listeners. It's the vibrant who, what, when, why, and where that makes the story stick. Stories don't tell facts as much as they illustrate them. The audience needs to see a picture, feel the conflict, in order to become involved in the story.

Not every listener will remember the same details. So, the communicator has to have enough color in their story that there will be something in it that is memorable for everyone.

If the sales group is sitting around talking the day after the morning session, someone will remember that Garrett tested out the demo with Scott, and someone else will remember that Scott has become a personal friend. Someone will focus on being surprised that Joe gave candid feedback, and someone else will remember Scott's line: "Can't take sales out of a leader."

As long as the communicator doesn't deviate from the central narrative and take a wild turn, most stories become much more interesting with color and embellishment that make details vivid and memorable.

This is an interesting point in the theory of art and science.

Communicators often tell me that they worry about their stories taking too long. In fact, participants in both our larger survey and our focus groups confirmed that this was a concern of theirs. Yet we've tested this out in our workshops, and the truth is that people are more worried about where the story is going than how much time it takes to get there.

When I teach programs on storylines and stories, I open the workshop with a story, and I try to stretch it out considerably to make sure that it takes me awhile to tell it. In the afternoon, when I refer back to my opening story as a way to discuss memorability, I ask the participants if they felt the story was too long. The answer is always no. When I ask what would make the story too long, groups almost always say if it got sidetracked or seemed to not be going anywhere.

So what I've found, is that if the length of the story comes from color commentary, adding texture around the characters and the setting, it doesn't feel long. Listeners are intrigued and entertained by the texture and embellishment of stories, especially when the communicators are a part of the stories themselves.

So, what about Mia's story?

- Will you remember that she reaffirmed two things: sales projections and consumer interest?

- Will you remember that the second point led the team deeper into the stats where they discovered that marketing groups represented over 40% of customer interest?

- Will you remember the hypothesis about bringing marketing into the conversation? Would you remember that one customer group felt your product would improve efficiency by 35%?

Or will you remember that her team is coming back in 30 days with a revised strategy?

My guess is that most people would remember the two data points within Mia's data story: 40% of customer interest came from marketing and one customer said that the product might deliver a 35% efficiency increase. Data is often used to make the data story memorable, and numbers are always more memorable when they are embedded in a story.

What if Mia had just stated that she had validation of a 35% increase in efficiency from a recent customer meeting? Without her set-up of the story, no one knows why the customer said that or why it was important to the overall strategy for the new product.

Mia could have built an experience story around the customer meeting, focusing only on the customer test that revealed the 35% efficiency boost. It's a compelling success story! But she knows that the biggest hurdle she needs to overcome is that the sales group is having a hard time trusting the data. So, she's smarter to stick with a data story that goes deeper to explain the disconnect.

Remember that the data stories stick to the facts and go narrower or deeper on observations, possibilities and assumptions about the data. These stories are built around a key challenge within the data that reveals new or evolving insights and helps listeners consider a new direction or trend. Even though these stories aren't as colorful as experience stories, they can still incorporate anecdotes about customer responses, industry trends, and macro- or micro-comparisons to ensure memorability and relevance.

Mia has two objectives in telling her story. She wants the sales group to know that the marketing group's insights were right, and the predictions for revenue are solid. But she also wants to expand their existing knowledge base so that they'll understand what can be done to improve results. She doesn't want to say or imply that her team structured the entire product launch incorrectly because this may demoralize the sales team. Instead, she needs to help the sales group solve for the disconnect between data and sales. Her story does a nice job of giving the group a new way of positioning the product and thinking about the needs within their customer base.

When we work with people to develop either type of story, we begin with building the structure and then ask for more detail to bring each phase to life. A colorful story will be remembered…but whether or not it will be repeated comes down to how the listener felt, not just what they remembered. The next chapter discusses injecting emotion into a story.

17

Pulling Emotion into Stories

In Chapter 14, I called emotion the blind spot for most storytellers.

It took me awhile to uncover it, but I believe that emotion is the element of stories that makes them repeatable. As I've studied stories and storytellers, I've traced stories to find the ones that have become company folklore or link people to the mission and culture of the companies they work for.

And my realization that emotion is often the missing piece came about in a rather funny way.

A few years ago, I was working with a new CEO on her year-end remarks. This young company has a well-loved tradition for how they "close" the year and celebrate their results.

For years, it all began with the company's founder. He would come to the central area of their workspace and bang on the table three times and then the floor two times to get everyone's attention. Then he would slowly look around and summon people to him with a direct stare or slow nod of his head. He caused a ripple of silence as employees jumped to attention. Pens dropped, chairs scraped and employees hustled to drop everything and gather in the center of the room to listen.

He would then shout phrases that summarized their successes that year and the employees would echo the phrases back to him. This was their rally cry, a source of inspiration.

Since the founder, every CEO would tell the first part of the story about the founder's intentional walk to the central space and then they would add their own phrases and echoed rally cry to summarize the current year.

The latest CEO that I was working with couldn't get the order of events straight in describing the founder's walk into the central area. She would say, "The founder walked to the central area and banged on the floor to get attention. Then, he waited until pens dropped and people stood and joined him in the center of the room." She could set up the feeling of tradition, but the company's communications person was distraught that she couldn't remember the proper order of the tradition.

He'd correct her: No...it's "pencils dropped, chairs scraped and first he has to summon them with a direct stare."

And she'd said it again: "He summoned them with a stare and they dropped pens and rolled their chairs trying to scurry to the center..."

The communications person wanted her to keep practicing the intro, but I knew she needed to spend time on the phrases that would become the rally cry of the current year and I was eager to help her get past this hurdle. So, I asked the communications person if the company was really hung up on the exact words and he was adamant that employees all knew the words by heart.

I suggested we walk around and let the CEO hear how others told the story; perhaps hearing them this way would help her understand the ritual of the words.

We walked around the floor and asked employees about the upcoming closeout of the year. I asked them to tell me what happens, and they all described the excitement of shouting out their successes and feeling like part of a team that verbally and loudly celebrates together.

Then, I asked about the setup of the story, and every single employee gave me a different synopsis of how the founder used to get the attention of employees. Some said he whistled, others said he banged a cane on the floor. Someone said pencils were thrown and someone else said employees raced in their chairs to the center of the room.

The CEO loved the variety in their stories because it proved her assumption. The employees were attached to the feeling of the ritual more than the literal words. When they had to repeat the story like she was going to do, they each remembered different details of it. But they could tell anyone about the event because they remembered the emotion they felt, and they could recreate it for someone else.

Nobody seemed unsure of the details as they shared them with me. Their accounts were confident and full of the emotion that the tradition evoked. Essentially, they were making up some of the details—without realizing it—to capture that emotion. They retold the story about the event to get me to feel the way that they feel every year.

And, that's how most people repeat stories. Think about that. You do it all the time in your personal life. Imagine your neighbor Tony comes over to tell you about another neighbor's annoying dog. He doesn't just tell you he's frustrated, but you see it when he walks you over to his shrub and, with great animation, convinces you it is destroyed. You go in your house and start the story by telling your spouse: "Boy, Tony's mad!" You share the emotion and then you tell them about the shrub.

We echo the emotion embedded in stories.

Garrett's experience story at the quarterly meeting was intentional about the emotion he wanted to evoke.

If Garrett wants his group to feel unsettled and unsure in their customer relationships, he may focus less on Joe and more on Scott and their relationship. He could retell the story to emphasize how comfortable he's become in the business relationship with Scott. He might describe the office and where he always sits, so that you'll pick up on familiarity and how well they know each other. That would make Scott's feedback even more surprising and drive home the idea that you may be missing something with your best customers. His unstated message might be that you're too comfortable and complacent about your customers.

But at this meeting, Garrett wants his team to feel a little vulnerable and open to feedback, and Joe plays an important role in setting that up. He's going to ask the team to give each other feedback, and he wants to illustrate his openness to feedback and Joe's willingness to give it. In his version of the story with the sales group, Joe is the most important character and the leader will spend time to help the sales group feel the struggle between him and Joe with the feedback that became the point of conflict.

As I've asked communicators about the emotion or feeling that they want their stories to create, most look at me like I'm crazy. The common responses are:

- "Well, it's my story, so I don't know that they will feel anything about it."

- "Emotion doesn't belong in a business setting."I don't want them to feel anything; I want them to do something."

I asked my list of great storytellers about emotion in their stories, and their answers were dramatically different.

- "Sure, I'm trying to elicit an emotion. I watch for it!"

- "Yes, emotion is at the root of every good story."

- "That's how I practice and improve stories. Thinking about the reaction I'm trying to get from listeners. I watch for the reaction and continue to work on stories to be sure that they're working for listeners."

Stories are all about feelings and emotions. That's why we love them and it's why we repeat them.

As I've studied stories and listened to how they travel across an organization, the details are often shuffled and even changed. The integrity of the story that remains is always the emotion that the listener felt and related to when they heard the story. They're good at repeating it because they're focused on sharing their reaction to the story. They may not own all the details, but they own the emotion, and the emotion is essentially what they are conveying.

So, how do you learn to transfer emotion?

We ask communicators to consider the emotion they want to evoke after they've outlined their story. It won't change the structure much, but it will influence the color commentary and the details that they choose to include. When a communicator focuses on how they want the listener to feel as they tell the story, the communicator works much harder on bringing emotion into the story and watching to see when a listener connects to it.

Telling a story with emotion tends to come naturally when it's a personal story that the presenter already feels an emotional connection to. But to get to the ability to evoke a specific emotion from an audience, it takes a confident and authentic communicator who's in tune with his or her audience enough to gauge their response and adjust in real time.

The communicator's ability to connect the story to a listener is more the art of style than the science of content. We'll look further at the storyteller's personal style skills in the final section of the book and Chapters 21-24.

But, before we leave stories, most communicators ask: Should stories be funny?

18

Humor in Stories

One request I often get when working with storytellers is: "I'd really like to be funny."

To which my response is, "Well…are you funny?"

The answer is always "no" because if they were funny they wouldn't be asking my permission to explore it. I understand why people want to be funny. Communicators want to use humor because they think it's an expectation of stories, and it's natural to crave the warm response that humor can draw from listeners.

But attempting to use humor and actually being funny are two very different things. We've all sat through meetings or speeches where the presenter makes jokes that come across as corny or forced. And, chances are, that presenter probably lost credibility because their attempt to connect felt inauthentic.

Humor increases the risks and rewards of engaging listeners in a business setting. Speakers who make others laugh are seen as self-confident and credible. But, our survey participants said that about a third of jokes are inappropriate in the workplace, and that brings considerable risks. The off-color story isn't the one that you want to be remembered for.

And, that may raise questions about what humor is. Humor is universal. It's an experience or a feeling that a room full of people can relate to in a similar way. Humor isn't sarcasm or a statement that calls out differences among people in a negative way.

Humor is a learned art form that can be used to create memorable sound bites and help endear an audience to a communicator. And it works! In fact, whenever we ask participants in our storytelling programs who they consider to be great storytellers, several people call out comedians. Ellen DeGeneres, Ron White, Chris Rock, Robin Williams, Stephen Colbert, Jimmy Fallon…the list goes on and on, and no matter the flavor or style of the comedian, what every listener will tell you is that the reason they laughed so hard and enjoyed the show, was because the comedian was believable. Audiences leave their shows saying, "Man, he/she just really gets it!"

But, it's hard to be funny and that's because…Humor is a unique blend of timing and authenticity.

I have coached people on timing. It isn't easy, but a person can learn to deliver a point on the right beat, in the right tone, and with emphasis on the best line. But timing alone is not enough. Humor really only works when it's authentic to the communicator.

This happens all the time in meetings, presentations, and keynotes, and more often than not, it's the main reason why attempts at humor can disappoint. When it's not your story, it's just not as funny.

Great comedians are funny because they take their own real, authentic, life experiences and turn them into stories we can relate to. They weave real pain, hope, love, and loss into their sets and that's why the jokes resonate with us.

We laugh at the description of someone's horrible blind date, because we've been on several ourselves. We laugh at the joke about the grill catching on fire because no one's Thanksgiving ever goes smoothly. Even when the show is over, the humor stays with us because we believed these stories and could see ourselves in them.

When people ask me to help them be funny, I do ask, "Well…are you funny?"

The truth is, if you are not naturally funny, using humor is going to be difficult. And when people aren't expecting it as a part of your brand, they might not respond well to it.

At the root of most peoples' desire to be funny is the desire to connect with our audiences. Laughing feels good and we think that if we can get our audience to laugh, then they will be in a good mood, they'll like us, and thus be more willing to listen to what we have to say. But for many speakers, humor feels awkward and even daunting to suddenly be relying on a punch line to earn the audience's favor.

And so when I'm asked about humor, I shift the focus from wanting to be funny to being authentic.

Imagine a VP of Information Technology, Ian, who has been asked to give the opening address for a conference on Smart City technology, and he opens like this:

> Every morning I take my dog Chessie for a walk around the block before I go to work, and on most days we'll see my neighbor and his dog Jet. Our two dogs always have to say hello to one another. Chessie is a Cockapoo, maybe about 5lbs or so, and Jet is a big Great Dane who weighs more than I do.

Apart from the very basic fact that they are both dogs, these two look like they would have no reason to talk to one another. They are practically different species. Yet, every day they communicate with one another and, presumably, pass information between themselves.

And watching my tiny Cockapoo pass information to a giant ten times her size got me thinking about the way we think about Smart Cities.

What if a street sign could communicate with your car?

What if a delivery truck could communicate with a cargo plane?

What if…

This isn't a funny story, but it's a real one. And, it's one that offers multiple opportunities for establishing a connection with the audience. Some people might own a dog themselves, and most can appreciate the image of a Great Dane socializing with a Cockapoo. Even if you knew absolutely nothing about Smart Cities before the speaker began, you now have a memorable frame of reference for some of the challenges the presenter will be addressing— how two seemingly disconnected things can connect in surprising ways.

Some people are naturally funny and bring a dry wit to most things they do. When we pick up on that in their brand, we encourage it because it is an authentic part of who they are.

If Ian is more comfortable using humor, he might tell the story this way:

Every morning when I get up, I lace up my running shoes, splash some cold water on my face, put my workout playlist on full volume, and take off running around the neighborhood with my wife's Cockapoo, Chessie. Yeah, I know. Me with a fluff-dog...it's a bad look. So is me running.

More often than not, while I'm trying to keep up with my wife's surprisingly swift fluffball, I usually run into my neighbor and his enormous Great Dane...Big Jet. Now, Jet's about the size of a horse, and my neighbor Ned is a very small guy. So, picture this. When Jet gets excited, he puts all that horsepower into full gear and starts barreling towards me and the fluffball with Ned flopping behind him like a paper flag.

And when this happens, I—on occasion—scream!

But Chessie doesn't. Somewhere in the recesses of this little fluffball's mind, she has identified Big Jet, aka Dogzilla, as a potential soul mate! And that really struck me as an incredible thing.

Here were two creatures, who to all of humanity are nothing alike, except for the broad fact that they are both (technically) dogs...at least my wife assures me that Chessie, is in fact, a real dog.

And this got me thinking about Smart Cities!

What if a street sign could communicate with your car?

What if a delivery truck could communicate with a cargo plane?

What if...

So if you've got the timing, and if humor is a part of how you see the world, go for it. Listeners will embrace it as part of their way of engaging your brand. Just be careful that it isn't the only element of your brand that people see and hear. There's a time to be funny and a time to be taken seriously. For most humorists, it's a fine balance.

If, on the other hand, humor is an art that you haven't yet mastered, focus a little less on the laugh and a little more on the connection. Connecting as a human is easier, if you are willing.

Listeners want to connect with you—your authentic self—in whatever form that takes for you. Successful stories are authentic ones, and in order for them to mean something to a listener, they first have to mean something to you.

19

Stories in Our Scenarios

We built out three storylines in the first portion of the book. I'll use the same scenarios to illustrate how a story can draw a listener into a topic.

SCENARIO #1: DATA SECURITY

Recall that Susan is a technology director whose responsibilities include data security protocol. To date, data security has been managed differently across her seven divisions. Her company recently introduced a new analytics product, SmartLine, which leverages data across all of the divisions. The company expects to drive over $200 million in new revenue because of it.

But the program also creates new risks as data moves across divisions. With all the additional access points, Susan predicts the risk of a breach would increase by as much as 20%. The company needs a new enterprise protocol to cover these access points before the analytics product launches. It won't be a welcome change because implementing the new protocol will disrupt the developers who are working to deliver the solution. Susan needs to recommend that all divisions halt development for 60 days to allow her to put a cross-divisional protocol in place.

Susan has unwelcome news and set the message of this storyline as:

If we delay the SmartLine launch for 60 days, we can adopt security protocols that will eliminate up to 20% added risk of a data breach.

There are at least two great options for stories in this scenario. Susan could use a story about a breach at another company to illustrate the increased risks and consequences associated with added capability. Or she could use a story to prove the data and explain the additional 20% risks in their network.

I'd add the following data story as context in the Situation phase of the storyline.

Scenario #1: Susan's Data Story

So, let me take a moment and explain the story behind the added risks.

When we began developing the SmartLine product, we had to remove the firewalls that exist in our network. We knew this at the time development began, and we were planning to rebuild the walls around the expanded network. But, we didn't scope a project plan around what would be required to do that.

Think about it this way. Imagine that you own a ranch and raise livestock on a hundred acres. You keep the livestock on your property, which is surrounded by stone walls. When those walls were built, you dug deep footers to set the walls and that's where your electrical wiring runs for lighting, alarms, and power around your property. At the time, it never occurred to you that you would move the walls or need to deconstruct any of this, and so the placement of those cables didn't matter.

Fast-forward several years. You now have an opportunity to buy your neighbor's land. It's another hundred acres that would expand your livestock business, and you jump at the chance. When your contractor draws up the plan to move the walls and double the size of your grazing field, you agree, and construction gets underway. The contracting team starts with the new wall and saves the demolition of the old wall as a final step, so the challenge with the electrical wiring isn't noticed until a later stage of the project.

That's a great way to think about what has happened with the SmartLine project. We focused on our stone walls and didn't know about the wiring that was buried beneath them.

So, here's the challenge. Our "wiring" is our SMB, or server message block. While we can move data through added access points already, we can't back-up our own data and we can't protect the data that we take in from clients to customize analytics. We need an enterprise system that allows us to secure and save data at each step. Since we weren't saving analytics during our testing phase, we didn't see the gap until a week ago.

We know where the weak links are in our fencing. We have eight access points that we're worried about. Those points represent 20% of the data power that support the new SmarkLink system, and they are at an increased risk today.

Our hypothesis is that we can rebuild two access points a week, which will take us a month. Then, we'll have 30 days to run the testing modules again and check the security of incoming data and our ability to save the combined analytics safely.

That's what we believe needs to happen and why we need 60 days to complete it.

Here's the second scenario with Bruce, who wants his team to accept change.

SCENARIO #2: CHANGE IN MANAGEMENT

Bruce leads a large division of a communications company, and he is responsible for bringing a new bundle of sports programs to market. Sports programming drives viewership three times higher than other programming, so it is a critical part of revenue planning and growth strategies. But sports viewers don't follow providers; they follow events. It's hard to capture their loyalty through a subscription. Bruce's team has an exciting idea to build participation into the sports bundle and allow subscribers to engage with each other in something like a fantasy league for each event. They believe that this could increase subscriptions by as much as 50%.

However, Bruce doesn't have the capability on his team to develop this interactive feature. It will require someone with strong gaming experience and expertise in real time technology. Bruce will have to get the product in the marketplace within six months or he'll miss the sales opportunity. He needs to hire two seasoned professionals who can develop the product in time. This won't be well received by his team. They've worked hard to come up with the concept and assess its potential. Bruce has told his leaders about this, but it will be a culture shift for an organization that typically promotes from within. He needs to talk to the entire team about the urgency of innovating quickly and the opportunity to bring in new skills and diversity of thought.

Bruce's message was:

By adding capabilities outside of our own experience, we can launch a sports package that could double subscriptions in six months.

The most compelling story for Bruce to use would probably be one that recounts his own experience with disappointment and how it impacted his career. Listeners appreciate a personal connection, especially if they perceive that the speaker has had a similar experience. It says "I know how you're feeling, because I've felt the same way."

I would encourage Bruce to open his storyline with a personal story similar to the one below.

Scenario #2: Bruce's Experience Story

Good morning! I hope that all of you are having a good quarter; I know that you're having a busy one! As we wrapped up the launch of this year's deliverables last quarter, I know that you've already begun your development meetings and early drafts of a roadmap for the new sports package. And in fact, it's the roadmap ahead of us that I want to talk to you about today.

Thinking about what I need to ask you to do on this project took me back to a time in my career when someone asked me to do something very similar.

I want to share that story as a prelude to what I'm going to ask of you today.

Twenty years ago, I was a young manager here and I was working hard to be successful in my role. I'd gotten a lot of positive feedback, and I was feeling confident about my ability to continue to grow within the company. I had a great mentor at the time, and he was helping me gain exposure to other leaders and more responsibility on larger projects.

I can still vividly remember what it was like in those days and how I felt after each project wrapped up. We delivered updates every quarter. For 18 straight months, I hit every deadline and even surpassed a few of the benchmarks. That's harder to do with the complexity of projects today, but we did it then, and I was quite proud of how my department was running.

I had several peers in the organization who also seemed to be getting more responsibility at about the same time as I was. And then a reorg came. We bought another company, and leaders decided to realign our divisions. It didn't take long to figure out this reorg was creating a new role at the division level....and I quickly got word that I was one of the managers they were considering for the job. I also learned that I was competing with Jane, a peer of mine, for this new leadership role.

It became more of a competition than it probably should have. My mentor was working hard to get support for me; her mentor was working hard to get support for her. Some of you have been in very similar situations. While you admire your peers, beneath it all you feel that you are the better candidate. I felt that way. I'd done everything right, and my team had outperformed other groups across the company.

I got a call from the division president, Paul, and he asked to meet with me on a Wednesday. I still remember it! I was sure that this was the moment. I would leave his office with a new title and a new role.

That's not what Paul asked of me, though. Instead, he told me that he was putting Jane in the role and he wanted me to understand why. Jane had some experience that I didn't have, and he felt that it would slow the business down if he let me learn that skill in the role. Jane also had some gaps, but he felt that, in this situation, her deficiencies would have less of an impact on the division. Paul told me that I had done everything right, he simply needed me to take one for the team. He went on to explain that highly valued leaders earned their stripes when they begin to put the company's needs ahead of their own. I didn't like Paul's message at the time…but I've never forgotten it.

Paul wasn't popular with my team that week…but he was right. Jane launched that new division and in two years it was one of the strongest in the company. But Paul never forgot what he'd asked of me. A year later, he came back and told me that it was my time to step up into a different opportunity, one that I was better suited for.

Last week, I asked the same thing of your leaders, and I'm going to ask all of you today to recognize what the business needs as we develop the new sports package.

My message to you today is similar:

We need to add capabilities outside of our own expertise in order to launch this product quickly and expand our own skills and capabilities in the year ahead.

That may not be how some of you envisioned moving forward with the sports package, but it's the right thing for the business. And, I'd like to spend time this morning explaining why I've come to that decision and what it will mean as we add new leaders to the team.

Here's the third scenario with Chandler, the salesperson who is trying to build credibility with prospective clients.

SCENARIO #3: CUSTOMERS & PRODUCTS

Chandler is a salesperson for a startup company, LoanLogic, that has developed an algorithm to qualify consumers for bank loans. It isn't a new concept. Financial institutions have several formulas to qualify loans. But LoanLogic has been able to bring personal analytics into the equation and can sync data from social media to profile people more effectively than a financial institution can.

Add to it a little sizzle and online interaction, and this tool may have great value to financial institutions who want to generate more loans. To prove the success of the algorithm and willingness of consumers to engage with the loan tool, LoanLogic set up smart kiosks in three shopping malls, positioned close to high-priced items like cars, jewelry, and electronics. The voice-activated kiosk drew a lot of attention and those who engaged the virtual loan officer completed the application process in under two minutes. The bank that piloted the kiosks with LoanLogic reported a 65% lift in loan applications and ultimately, a 50% increase in completed loans.

Chandler's next step is to get banks to purchase the product, which can then be applied to their website or positioned as a free-standing kiosk like the one LoanLogic put in shopping malls. How will Chandler position the product?

Chandler's message was:

By implementing our two-minute tool, you can increase loans by 50%.

The best use of a story in Chandler's case would be a customer success story. We would add this to the Solution segment of his presentation as one of the case studies.

Here's how that story might go.

Scenario #3: Chandler's Experience Story

One of our customers transitioned to self-service lobbies five years ago. They have leveraged a lot of automation through virtual tellers and 24/7 access to their lobbies. In fact, they've built an entire marketing campaign around the ease of banking with them. Since the transition, they've seen account openings increase and traffic in these lobbies pick up as much as 30%, mostly in the evening hours between 7–10pm.

Their customer surveys showed a very positive response to the self-service features until a year ago. They launched a major loan initiative, and customers didn't find the loan process easy or accessible. The bank saw negative feedback on social media and on their surveys about false promotion of their brand and how hard it was to get a loan with them.

The bank's loan process wasn't actually all that different from that of most banks, but it isn't easy. The process is slow and requires a lot of data entry. Their incomplete rate is more than 50%. They heard about our kiosk and reached out to see if it was a fit.

Turns out it's more than a fit. For the last six months, we've had our kiosk set up in the self-service lobby. One out of four people engage with it during their visit. It's become an entertainment draw because the kiosk stays active and "talks" to people who get near it. We've been able to capture data about the lobby visits as well as the loan process itself.

The bank's loan applications are up by 50% and they have completed more than 25% of those loans to date. Social media chatter about their brand is back to positive as well. It's even become a popular item to "find" on local scavenger hunts. We've helped the bank increase loans, restore their reputation, and continue to make financing fun and easy.

You've seen each of these scenarios unfold throughout the book. The storyline is well-developed, and the message is strong enough in each scenario to peak the interest of the listeners. In all three examples, the communicator has all the right elements to complete the journey that they've laid out for the listeners.

But, the addition of the stories above pulls the listeners deeper into the storyline and creates a stronger connection to the experience or insights of the communicator. Listeners aren't just agreeing with a message; they now have a memorable element from the presentation that they're likely to repeat. This changes the impact of the communicator significantly. If the listeners in each scenario leave the discussion and share these stories, they build momentum for the proposed outcome and help the communicators gain leverage across an organization or in a customer situation.

That's one of the insights that great storytellers have, and you'll read more of their lessons learned in the next chapter.

20

Lessons from Storytellers

We have a wall of great storytellers in our office; some of the faces are recognizable but many are not. Few business people are celebrities. I like that. It validates that you don't have to lead a company or be on the front page of the Wall Street Journal to be a great storyteller.

When I began working on this book, I sought out the storytellers that I knew and studied their habits to get to the core of what makes a great storyteller.

Here are my observations and the combined thoughts of 100 storytellers that we interviewed.

The Use of Stories

"Use stories to connect to the listener and reinforce a point. Stories make content easy to track. Listeners can follow where you're going, and stories can get people to think or feel a certain way."

"People want to know that you're human, and we are all fascinated with personal stories. People like humility and mistakes."

"Stories belong in business because business is about influencing. The fastest way to influence someone is to connect via empathy and emotion."

"Stories can be a window into a culture… they can empower people to do things they may not think they are capable of."

I learned that great storytellers tell stories all the time. Stories show up in letters, in emails, through videos, and on stage. They tell stories one-on-one, to small groups and large audiences. They use stories to show their vulnerability, share what they've learned, and help people see things differently.

The Model of Stories

"To build a story, you have to understand the mindset of the listener. Listeners need to be able to imagine themselves in your story."

"You have to be purposeful about translating stories and map out how an idea will be compelling to others. It's not about what I think; it's what will make you think."

"There is a skill and an order to telling a story. You have to create an experience and lead listeners to an amazing discovery."

"You have to stay on track. Stories have to drive to a point and storytellers need to know where the ending is."

Even the most experienced storytellers are intentional about the flow of the story. Most say that they practice stories a lot before presenting them. I shared our model of Structure + Interest + Emotion, and it was overwhelmingly endorsed by all of them.

Storytelling Can Be Taught

"Storytelling is a teachable skill. You can get better with practice. You have to understand how your voice and body work to tell a story well."

"You have to understand empathy. Stories are designed to draw response and reaction from listeners."

"I think you evolve as a storyteller. As a young leader, my messages were always fact based. As I've evolved as a communicator, I've gotten much better at pulling listeners into the content."

Some of the storytellers I interviewed have been telling stories for more than 40 years, others less than a decade, and some just started in the last year. A few learned the skill from a grandparent. Storytelling is an art that has been passed down from generation to generation to preserve family history and life lessons. Some talk about intentional choices they made to learn how to tell stories; others have developed enough of a habit around it that they associate storytelling with their confidence as a communicator.

When Stories Don't Work

I asked storytellers for their observations about what goes wrong when a story doesn't work.

"Stories don't work when someone is scared or appears as if the story was forced on them."

"When the storyteller is too nervous to be real or doesn't feel authentic."

"When it's the wrong story and the wrong group. Stories must transfer to listeners. It may be a good story but if it remains my story, it doesn't work."

Their observations matched up with our larger survey: stories don't work when the storyteller isn't involved in telling the story.

When Stories Are Told Well

"I can feel it when it works. When I tell a story well, there's an energy exchange."

"Stories simplify ideas, and listeners let you know that they understood the idea."

"Stories evoke something. Stories are a way to find commonality with a listener, and then you go somewhere together."

"You light up when you tell a story. You're excited to tell it and are eager to see how it will be received. It's the best part of the storyline."

Great Stories Are Memorable

"It's the emotional connection that's memorable."

"I hear stories retold that I shared years ago. People remember the personal parts of your story and reconnect with you on those."

"I hear my stories repeated a lot and some of them are more than 10 years old."

"No one ever reads the exact book I wrote. A novel is a conversation between the author and the reader. But it becomes the story that they want to read, and they repeat it a little differently. That's proof that the story resonated with them."

I was interested in tracing the lifeline of stories in companies. Stories often have remarkable longevity, especially when a company culture has strong ties to its founder.

One storyteller shared his experience of working for a company during a tough time with product delivery and customer satisfaction. Employees wanted to hear the honest story about the gaps in their products and their customers' frustrations. But, none of the leaders wanted to tell it. So, he did. He spoke candidly about what they were doing wrong, and his story of customer frustration and product shortcomings got employees engaged. He quickly became the designated storyteller in the company culture.

Finding Stories

"Stories are within you and in your life. The best stories are inside of us: our personal challenges and experiences."

"Books are full of stories. I write down stories that I read and keep them as future material."

"Stories can come from topics that you like. I'm fascinated by how companies get started, and I've collected stories about companies that I use frequently."

"Stories are everywhere. I listen and ask questions so that I can tell other people's stories. Pay attention to your world."

"A lot of communicators spend too much time on facts to back up their thoughts, but the great ones spend more time on stories to establish trust and a more emotional connection with listeners."

As you can see, confident storytellers don't worry about where to find material. They've learned to listen and collect ideas and stories along the way. And, the willingness to do that is a differentiator for storytellers.

People often tell me that they don't have any stories. When I recommend they share something from their personal life, they're hesitant, and when I suggest that they reach out to a few listeners to see if there's a story within the group, they say they don't have time.

I wonder what their listeners would say if they heard the lack of willingness or the lack of time from the communicator. I think they'd say if the communicator doesn't have time to make it relevant and compelling, then don't communicate.

Great storytellers work hard at this. They invest in building strong storylines and finding just the right stories that will be remembered and repeated.

The Style of Storytellers

"Inspiring storytellers are inspired themselves. The eyes are expressive, the voice changes, and the emotion can be seen and heard."

"Good storytellers are at ease. They use physical cues to add dimension to a story. A little acting and involvement makes it more fun."

"Great storytellers use a lot of silence. Words seem to have more impact surrounded by silence."

"Storytellers have a natural enthusiasm and are very expressive when they tell a story."

"It takes energy to pull something out of a listener."

"It's all about style: it's timing, pace, pause, and vocal expression."

This brings us to the final section of the book: the style of storytellers. While some of the magic of storytelling evolves with practice, there are fundamental skills that we can use to help a communicator develop to become more confident and expressive and really win at telling stories.

Section 4

The Magic of Storytellers

21

The Power of Impressions

Every interview I had with the storytellers from the previous section included a discussion of their delivery skills. As accomplished storytellers, they have intention behind their styles and feel very much at ease with any group, but they remember a time when it wasn't always so. They remember becoming more aware of the impact of style, and they relate to every nuance of building confidence and engaging an audience.

While the storytellers I interviewed didn't claim to be masters of style, I've seen all of them as presenters and they command a room and consistently pull listeners into what they're saying. They did acknowledge the effort and feedback it took to get their communication skills to where they are today.

Communicators focus first on how they're seen and heard by listeners, and then they shift to what draws the listener into their storyline. Before you can become a compelling communicator, you have to feel like a competent one.

Let's go back to the listeners' perspective and their expectations about communication style and impact. The power of impressions and the quick rate at which they form was documented in my first book.

In seven seconds, people form 11 impressions of a communicator. Because impressions are quick, they are strongly rooted in how listeners see and hear you. Here are the facts:

- 55% of an impression is based on physical posture.

- 38% of an impression is based on the sound of your voice.

- And 7% of an impression is based on the actual words you speak.

So, while the storyline is critical to get a listener to follow you, your style has to engage the listener before the storyline is even set up.

A compelling storyteller has executive presence. And, I would say that executive presence is how listeners experience storytellers, and listeners are clear about their expectations of those impressions and that experience.

In our workshops, we ask participants to build a list of expectations and attributes they associate with presence. Their lists are always remarkably similar. Here are the most common expectations:

Confident	Enthusiastic	Genuine	Connected
Comfortable	Involved	Clear	Sincere
Credible	Aware	Vested	Authentic
At Ease	Passionate	Thoughtful	Interesting

That's a daunting list for any communicator…until they understand how to deliver on them. And, that's where our work begins. We help communicators understand how impressions are shaped by the use of the body and voice, and how to make intentional choices that strengthen initial impressions.

There are three overarching attributes that we use to represent all of the others, and we call them the three C's of style: Confidence, Commitment, and Connection.

Confidence: A confident communicator is someone who seems comfortable, relaxed and open. They seem at ease with listeners in any setting and that ease makes them appear clear, credible and knowledgeable, as if they have the right to be there. We coach confidence as a physical feeling, and we work with clients on posture, grounding, and other ways that they can influence the physical space around them. This group of attributes drives 55% of an initial impression and the physical posture mentioned above.

Commitment: A committed communicator is someone who brings energy to their thoughts. They are passionate about their ideas, which in turn makes them interesting to listen to. Listeners describe them as enthusiastic, involved and vested in their thoughts. We coach commitment as effort and the best use of the voice, and we work with clients on articulation, projection, and inflection to create warmth and interest behind their words. This group of attributes aligns to 38% of initial impressions and the sound of the voice mentioned above.

When communicators understand how to use the body and voice effectively, they become more competent. And because those attributes drive 93% of an initial impression, they are critical to learn. When someone can't use their voice and body well, it's hard to stay focused on them long enough to hear much of what they say.

But, the ultimate goal for a communicator is to feel competent enough to focus their attention on the listener. And, that's when they become compelling.

Connection: A connected communicator is someone who is focused on the listeners' reaction and response. The focus shifts from how the communicator is doing to how the listener is feeling. The connected communicator is actively involved with a group and seems to be working to draw every listener into a conversation. This effort and engagement leads to impressions of trust, sincerity, and authenticity. Connection is what keeps an audience engaged beyond the initial impressions formed by a speaker's confidence and commitment.

In the next three chapters, I'll share the coachable concepts that help communicators deliver on these expectations of their personal style.

22

Coachable Skill – Confidence

Body language determines the largest portion of listeners' first impressions. Even if your body signals aren't intentional, it's hard for a listener to get beyond what they think your posture and your body are expressing. Posture means more than how you stand or look. It's awareness of how you use your body to convey a sense of openness, settled-ness, and focus for the listener.

When we ask people to define executive presence, some of their favorite expressions are, "You know it when you see it" or, "There are some people who just own a room." Both expressions are a reaction to the physical-ness of someone.

In our presence workshops, we introduce body language as both a mental and physical choice. Communicators have to mentally agree to be the center of attention before we can coach them on conveying confidence physically. For many people, the concept of being open translates to being vulnerable. And that vulnerability is very real. Being the focal point for a room full of listeners can make a communicator feel exposed.

But remember the descriptions of the compelling storyteller. Listeners like people who are willing to be vulnerable with them. We like people who seem at ease with our attention and seem to be working to turn it into a real connection.

This starts with the physicality of communication.

How should you use your body to convey a sense of confidence? How does your body say, "I'm comfortable. I know what I'm talking about."

We coach five steps of posture to achieve this:

First: the width of the feet. The width of your feet should match the width of your armpits. When your stance is too narrow, it makes you unsteady. When the stance is too wide, it pulls you back and away from listeners, which makes you appear stiff.

Second: balance evenly on both feet. Many people shift their weight around when standing in front of a group. It's unintended movement, but it can quickly become something that people watch about you, instead of listening to you. Your balance has to be steady and evenly distributed on both feet. When the posture sways or shifts in front of a group, it can send signals to your listeners that you're nervous or unsure of your material.

The lower part of the body is about owning the space and feeling grounded and solid. That heaviness conveys a communicator's right to be there and helps them own the space more effectively than someone who seems to stay in motion or unsettled on their feet.

Then, the next three steps of posture shift to the upper body.

Third: core engagement. This concept can feel odd to communicators until they understand the intent behind it.

When you communicate 1:1 with someone, you actually bring the core of your body toward them. Think about how you shake hands with a person. You move the core of your body closer to them, not just your hand. When communicators stand in front of a group, they need to incorporate the same concept. The use of the core of the body is a big component of getting physically involved in communication. Remember that many storytellers are animated. The physical-ness that listeners notice the most is the core of the upper body active in getting a point across.

Fourth: open and relaxed arms. Most communicators find their arms a nuisance and wish they could forget about them when they're speaking. They worry too much about what their hands are doing and they often end up closing off the upper body by locking their hands in front of them or crossing their arms because they don't want their hands to be too demonstrative. You should use your arms naturally. They can't be locked in front of you, because it limits your involvement in what you're saying, and listeners read that body language as closed, uninvolved and uncomfortable being the focus of their attention.

Fifth: a level head. When the body shifts, the head can tilt as well and this causes a look of uncertainty.

The five steps of posture also apply to a seated stance. When you sit down behind a desk or across a conference table, steps one and two are no longer challenges. Your center of gravity is much lower which makes the choices with the feet and legs less significant. But, steps three-five become more important as the upper body is often the only portion that a listener can observe.

Core engagement is a critical part of seated communication. In fact, we expect to see someone come forward when they speak from a seated position. When we don't see this, we assume the communicator isn't vested in what they're trying to say. The arms frame the space, and we read open shoulders and open hands as a signal that someone is receptive to discussion. The level head has the same impact seated or standing.

Being comfortable or confident is a physical feeling. As we work with people to own their space, we help them think about balance and finding a lower center of gravity so that the body doesn't just look settled and solid, but really is more grounded. These physical concepts are about building muscle memory and developing habits that you can rely on every time you're speaking.

Confidence is the boldest of all the attributes of presence. There's nothing you can say that will override what the body says to listeners. Knowing how to use the body well helps many communicators feel at ease and in command of a room.

23

Coachable Skill – Commitment

The listener feedback from our research in Chapter 2 was that listeners prefer storytellers who make content interesting versus brief. Listeners want communication to make a point, but they also like getting involved with the message and feeling like they're part of it.

That takes effort from a communicator. It requires energy and investment to make people want to sit up and listen. We like to experience communicators who are working to share information with us.

So, how do communicators do this?

It's about how they communicate more than what they communicate. We see animation or physical involvement from communicators, and we don't always recognize that it's driven by the effort behind their words. You won't see a physically involved communicator who mumbles or is hard to understand. When communicators say it like they mean it, they begin to use their bodies to support the conviction that they're feeling.

While the body gives the first impression, the voice does most of the work after that. The harder a communicator works to make a point, the more involved the body becomes in the effort.

How do you add more strength to the voice?

There are three fundamental technical skills: articulation, projection and pause.

Articulation drives the effort behind the voice. It involves the use of the whole mouth, shaping the words for clarity and energy. You can observe articulation if you stand in front of a mirror and try this simple exercise:

- Watch yourself as you say the sentence: "I need the report at two o'clock."

- What you'll see the first time is your normal energy level.

- Now, mix it up a bit.

- Repeat and watch as you say the sentence very monotone, with no effort or inflection behind the words.

- Now repeat and watch as you say it with a lot of effort behind the words.

If you repeat the low and high-energy deliveries a few times, you'll notice that the monotone sentence shows no expression or interest on the face. Whereas the high effort sentence shows expression through your whole face.

Articulation drives expression, and as listeners, we like communicators who are expressive when they speak. Expressive communicators are more interesting and easier to listen to. Even when our hearing isn't impaired, everyone reads lips a bit when we can look at a communicator. And the more effort we see, the more commitment we believe.

If you're guilty of using too many words to make a point,

articulation also helps eliminate filler or unnecessary words. When we coach communicators to articulate, we find that they reduce their word count because they're focused on putting effort behind each word.

The second skill we coach is **projection**.

Projection is the intention of getting the voice forward when you speak. It's the difference in a listener who feels as if you're talking at them versus talking with them.

Projection starts with voice placement. Some people keep their voice in the back of the throat, which can result in a guttural or thin and raspy sound. It may be caused by tightness in the chest or just the habit of keeping the voice back. In most cases, the voice can be released and brought forward for a fuller tone.

Projection begins by getting the voice toward the front of the mouth. You can feel this by humming. When you hum, your mouth is closed, and you should feel a slight vibration on your lips.

Try this simple exercise to ensure that the voice is in the front of the face. Hum for about two seconds and then say a number as you open your mouth. "Mmmmm…one."

We describe this position of the voice as "out." You can feel the voice in the front of the face and you could feel the voice expressed out in front of you as you said the number. This cleans up the guttural or raspy sounds in voices that are held back.

Most people speak with the voice out. They can easily feel the voice in the front of the face and they assume that projection means just talking louder. But, projection is a step beyond the space right in front of you. Projection is the intent to get the voice forward to wherever your listener is. Everything about good communication focuses forward, toward the listener, rather than holding back, concentrating on the communicator.

Here's a way you can experiment with projection:

- Find a room in your house or an empty conference room in your office.

- Using the full length of the room, line up chairs in three positions. The first chair should be close to you, the second chair should be half the distance of the room from you, and the third chair should be as far away from you as the length of the room allows.

- Stand in one spot and think about placing your voice in each chair. You can use numbers to get a feel for the exercise. Place "one" in the first chair, "two" in the second, and "three" in the third.

- Begin again by placing "four" in the first chair and so forth.

If you continue the exercise as you count to twenty, you will notice that it takes more effort to get the voice to the third chair. If you incorporate the physical concepts discussed in the previous chapter, you should be able to feel the effort to project pulling the upper body forward. Projection drives core involvement.

When we project or place the voice with a listener, we align the core of our body with them as well. The voice and body are forward to the listener, and this is what creates the listener's feeling that someone is talking to them.

Both of these technical skills help a communicator convey the attributes of commitment. Articulation drives the energy and effort behind words, showing the speaker's investment in them. Projection gets the words forward to listeners, indicating the speaker's deference to the listener.

So, it may come as a surprise that a third vocal technique that we coach is **silence**.

Great storytellers use pauses effectively. Pauses give listeners a chance to catch up. They convey intentionality. Great storytellers use silence to pull listeners along the storyline and add intrigue. You'll notice that great storytellers pause at just the right moment. They watch to see when you are intrigued and then they pause the story so that you're eager for the rest of it and are right in-step with where they're going next.

Using the body and voice effectively, require new skills and building good habits. And once we build confidence and commitment in the communicator's skill set through effective use of the body and voice, we shift their focus to connecting with listeners.

24

Coachable Skill – Connection

When we described the attributes of executive presence, there were some attributes that were more emotional: authentic, honest, sincere and trustworthy. These illustrate a shift from how the listener feels about the communicator to how the communicator makes the listener feel.

In our workshops, we illustrate the concept of connection in 1:1 conversations. Most of us know how to connect with individuals, and we do it easily when we're talking to one person. The challenge comes when speaking in front of a group and learning how to connect with multiple people all at once.

Many communicators think that connecting with an audience requires a different approach than connection to a single person in a face-to-face conversation. They talk about scanning the room, glancing in a general direction, or looking over people's heads toward the back of the room. The problem with these techniques is that they defeat the point of connection—that is, to read the interest and reaction of each listener. That's not something that can be done with a glance, and it certainly can't be done if you're looking at the clock on the back wall to avoid making eye contact.

Eye contact is a part of Connection, but Connection is more than looking at people. It includes an awareness of and interpretation of non-verbal cues and responses from listeners. Connection continues to happen at a 1:1 ratio even in groups. We coach communicators to rethink how they connect with a group of a hundred people. It is never 1:100 or a communicator talking to one hundred people at the same time. It is always 1:1....100 times which means a communicator talking to individuals in the group and connecting one at a time with a hundred of them.

As groups get larger, communicators grow increasingly skeptical of this technique. But it works. You've probably experienced it firsthand. A good communicator can make it seem, in a room of a thousand people, as if they are talking to you. And, the reason is that connection is occurring. While a communicator may not literally be able to see 1,000 people, they can make 1,000 people feel seen. And, it's because they continue to talk to individuals, which creates expression on the communicator's face that illustrates a conversational and authentic level of engagement. Listeners recognize that and respond to it.

I've talked a lot about vulnerability and confidence in personal styles, and connection is the group of attributes that challenge a communicator the most. It means that the communicator has to feel confident enough in their own habits and impressions to shift their focus to the listener. It means standing in front of groups or speaking up in meetings and thinking less about how you're doing as a communicator and more about how the listener is feeling and reacting.

That shift in focus is difficult for communicators to make, but it is the differentiating skill that great storytellers have mastered.

I'm often asked how all three of the attributes of presence show up in companies, and this is what I've observed for many years.

Confidence is the boldest group of attributes. Because of that, I describe confidence as table stakes in companies. Leaders must have confidence to lead people. Companies hold potential leaders back when they don't have it, and they pull people forward who do have it. It is not only a communication skill, but it is an essential skill and expectation of leadership.

Commitment is the most varied group of attributes. Communicators don't always understand how to use the voice and they may stop short of trying to improve it. In many companies, I see some leaders who are confident but not very interesting. Listeners notice this. They are less interested in seeing the low energy leader take the stage or lead the meeting. In fact, it can be the point at which one leader gains more visibility than another because companies like to put the more interesting communicators in the spotlight.

Connection is the most compelling group of attributes. When listeners talk less about their impressions of a communicator and more about their connection to a communicator, it's a clear signal that they've engaged with the communicator and the storyline. While connection can feel like an elusive skill to develop, it brings the attributes of presence that listeners admire most in leaders. When authenticity and sincerity show up in a leader's style, companies recognize that these communicators can influence their listeners.

It takes all three attributes to drive impact. It takes confidence to earn the right to speak, commitment to build interest, and connection to engage listeners in the storyline. When a communicator understands how to deliver on all of these attributes, a master storyteller emerges.

But, as you've heard all of the components, you may still have questions about challenges you haven't overcome as a communicator. There are three common roadblocks that most communicators ask about: being open as an introvert, managing and overcoming nerves, and connecting with a remote audience. I'll answer those questions in the following chapters.

25

Introverts as Storytellers

There are many great storytellers who would say they are introverts. And that surprises a lot of self-proclaimed introverts who view compelling communication as a strictly extroverted skill.

But, I hope this book has proven that there aren't innate storytellers or natural communicators. There are people who have elements of natural skill in how they communicate, and many effective communicators have honed innate skills to develop consistency. But every great communicator and storyteller agrees: good storytelling takes practice.

The question about communication as an extrovert's skill usually comes from someone who considers themselves an introvert. And, it always seems to start from a place of hoping that there's some way to communicate without having to feel as vulnerable and as open as the elements of style suggest. Many introverts hope that words will be enough, but words alone are not the value or the goal of spoken communication.

While I have great empathy for the hard work it takes to learn effective communication, I tell everybody the same thing: it's not about you. Spoken communication is not about what's happening with you, it's all about what's happening for your listener.

That's a tough message to hear if you'd prefer to sit in the back of the room rather than stand in the front of it. I've worked with many introverts over the years, and none of them were eager to step into the limelight. But understanding the intention behind communication and the impact of organizing a message from the listener's perspective has helped hundreds of reluctant communicators find their voice.

For the introvert, some of the concepts I've discussed throughout this book are more overwhelming than others. Building a connection with a live audience can seem daunting and sharing a personal story can seem too revealing. But even the most reluctant communicators can become strong communicators. The key is to understand how introverted habits can be modified to drive compelling communication.

Here are the common things that introverts say when they hear the style concepts and coaching techniques that we've discussed.

"I don't like being the center of attention." When someone is uncomfortable being in the spotlight, the audience can literally see it. Uncomfortable communicators' shift their weight, close their stance, clasp their hands and cross their arms as if to block their exposure to the audience. These aren't intentional or deliberate choices as much as they are a reflex and reaction to the feeling of exposure.

I build confidence in an introverted communicator by shifting their focus from how the body feels to how the body looks to others. Videotaping is a great technique to help people see the impact of an open body and a more inviting physical posture. Everyone likes how it looks; then it's just a matter of getting comfortable with how it feels.

The body and physical posture adjust easily to new choices and seeing confidence as an impression helps someone feel confident as a communicator. The five elements of posture that I described in Chapter 22 help build the physical choices. In short order, the more open stance actually feels more confident than the initial choices of a closed body.

Some of the introvert's worries about the body come from misconceptions about how to get there. While some communicators combine movement and motion into their body language, it isn't necessary and sometimes it's even inappropriate. A communicator doesn't have to be the energizer bunny in front of a group. Remember that energy comes from the voice, not body motion. Every communicator can learn to project a settled body and a calm and open demeanor.

"Energy is exhausting." It certainly can be if you have to speak to a large group or for an extended period of time. It often helps introverted communicators to think about energy as less of a performance and more about the intention of getting a point across.

Coaching commitment is similar to coaching confidence. It's important to hear the impact in order to buy into the change. Often, introverts are more soft-spoken. Articulation and projection help someone hear the tentativeness in a softer tone and enable a communicator to strengthen their voice by focusing it forward.

My goal is to make sure a communicator's energy level is enough to keep the interest of listeners, and it takes practice to help a communicator adjust to hearing their voice differently.

Content can help build energy and interest with listeners, and we often help a more reluctant communicator find creative ways to bring energy into the talk track. We use video, audience participation, and group exercises to help a less dynamic speaker carry a room.

"Everyone wants a piece of me." Yes, they do! If you're the communicator, people want to connect with you. Introverts can be very good at 1:1 engagement; but like most communicators, they just don't transfer that to a larger setting. And, the coaching is the same as the concept I described in Chapter 24—you're not talking to a group of a hundred people. You're talking to one person, a hundred times.

The difference in connection for an introvert lies in the elements of their personality that may have labeled them as an introvert to start with. I'm sure I oversimplify the distinction between an extrovert and an introvert by describing my observations of how they manage energy. Extroverts get energized from other people. Introverts restore their energy with solitude. Extroverts find talking to a large group energizing; introverts find it exhausting. Extroverts enter a room and want to shake every hand; introverts are more comfortable talking to a few people and staying on the outskirts of the larger group. These are distinct personality types, and neither is better than the other.

But, communication requires connection, and most communicators have to learn how to manage the demands of that connection.

Whenever I meet a more introverted communicator who seems convinced that they'll never be able to get up on a stage or win over a room, I remind them that growth isn't about changing who they are. It's about modifying habits and strengthening their style to meet the listeners' expectations.

26

Speaking Gets on My Nerves

For some communicators, the biggest hurdle to storytelling is nerves.

Speaking really can get on our nerves. People say that it makes them physically uncomfortable, makes them vulnerable and, given the choice, it's something that most would gladly pass to someone else to handle.

And in a business setting, I've heard hundreds of attempts to do just that.

- "Don't you think I could just send this via email and let people read it for themselves?"

- "How about I tell the group that I'm uncomfortable and don't enjoy talking to people?"

- "I want to be sure my team gets visibility, so I'm going to 'let' someone else present this."

- "This wasn't in my job description. I don't think I should have to do it."

- "I'd rather just answer questions. Can't they just ask questions?"

I've heard it all. And, I recognize most strategies to get out of the spotlight.

Most communicators experience nervous energy when they speak. You get more juice in your system when you know you have to get a point across clearly. That's adrenaline, and it's as common as the physical lift you feel during an exercise class, winning a hard chess match, or celebrating an exciting moment with friends.

But that isn't what some people mean when they ask us about nerves. They mean a more anxious feeling, and they experience physical responses that feel more out of control and less desirable than the adrenaline rush of a physical activity. That isn't uncommon either, although it is something that you can work through and learn to manage effectively.

When we talk to people about feeling anxious or nervous, we describe the cause of nerves as both a mental state and a physical state. One is the cause of anxiety and the other is the manifestation of it.

In order to take the stage, you may need some techniques to manage through nerves.

Why We Feel Nervous – Mental State

While I am not qualified to diagnose clinical anxiety, I've worked with people on nerves enough to know that how you're thinking drives how you're feeling.

And when someone wants to work on nervous feelings, I begin by talking to them about what they're thinking. Many communicators put a lot of pressure on visibility moments, and some can work themselves into thinking that speaking is more than just a moment in time. Instead, it becomes a suspended amount of time that they're not sure they can get through or cope with. When I hear a situation described as bigger than it should be, I know that there may be some anxiety attached to it.

I encourage people to talk to a physician about it and learn more about dealing with anxiety. This may mean recognizing nervous feelings aren't just linked to an upcoming speaking situation. Sometimes multiple factors can contribute and there are a number of worries to work through before the present anxiety can be overcome.

And, sometimes anxiety is tied to a stressful period of life. I see this and hear about this more often than I used to. In our efforts to go fast, work effectively, and blend all elements of our lives together, we don't always give ourselves a release valve. And the way we're feeling and thinking usually shows up in our body and voice.

Case in Point: I coached a woman recently who was working on a big presentation. We had developed her storyline, and she felt good about the content two weeks before she delivered it. But when I followed up with her later, she told me that she hadn't delivered it well and she was certain it was because she got nervous in the middle of it. I hadn't seen much of this in our rehearsal sessions, so I asked her more about it. With a little probing, I learned that she had been traveling non-stop for twelve days prior to the presentation. She'd had the flu the previous week and had been taking over the counter flu medication for four days. She had gone to dinner the night before with a client and stayed out late. She was so exhausted that after the meeting, she went home and slept for two days. She was nervous, but she was also run down, exhausted and dehydrated. She didn't make the connection between the anxious feeling and her physical state.

How We Feel Nervous – Physical State

Regardless of what causes nervous feelings, nerves manifest themselves in a physical or a vocal response. And in most cases, that's something we can either solve for or help someone understand how to deal with in the moment.

To minimize the manifestation of nerves, we observe someone's communication style. We watch the use of the body and we listen to the quality of the voice. Nerves will show up in physical tightness and voice restrictions, and we can help someone feel and see those symptoms occurring. People carry their bodies differently and they use their voices differently. So, solving for nerves isn't a one size fits all approach. But, here are a few concepts that nervous communicators can use to improve how they feel and sound.

The Body –When someone feels nervous, they may shift their weight, rub their arm, clasp their hands or any number of unintentional movements. This tightens the body and can make you appear rigid, withdrawn, tight and uncomfortable which most people say they are.

As we discussed with the introvert, we solve for these unintentional choices by helping people become more aware of the use of the body. A nervous body can feel out of control, so it helps to have a better understanding of a grounded stance and to learn how to feel settled on your feet.

We also teach two techniques to help a communicator release nervous energy before their speech or presentation begins.

The first technique is a physical release of muscles. The most visible signs of nerves are often in the shoulders and through the core of the body. Communicators can release this by swinging the arms and moving the core of the body around to release the shoulders. This helps start from a more neutral place rather than a tight place. Before a speaking event, find a private space in the restroom or outside a ballroom to physically release the core of your body and relax.

The second technique is being intentional about how communication begins. Nervous communicators say they feel more nervous at the start of the speech and seem to relax toward the middle. And, some of that initial nervousness comes from a lack of direction about how to begin. The storyline and the message help the content start intentionally, and we coach communicators on simple techniques to feel settled in their stance and connected to the listener before the content begins.

The Voice: When the body tightens, the voice retreats. It's harder to focus on these signs, because you can't see them; you have to hear them instead. Communicators may pull the voice back unintentionally or habitually, which makes it sound thin, tight and even gruff. That's nerves, and it's caused by tightening in the body discussed above.

The voice exercises I highlighted in Chapter 23 can free the voice and build a fuller quality to someone's voice. And through coaching, we can help someone learn to hear the difference and work through a more tense or tight moment. Our techniques are specific to how the voice is trapped, but the common cause of voice constraint is usually a physical change: tight shoulders, closed arms, or a pulled-back core.

The overall coaching is to remember that the body owns comfort and confidence. The more relaxed the body, the fuller the voice.

If nervous energy is your roadblock, don't give up on becoming an effective communicator. Mastering communication can be a challenge, but it can also be your greatest asset. It takes a little help to understand what nervous energy really is and why it may be occurring. But with the right tools and a little practice, the situation that you dread the most can become the skill that actually gets you ahead.

27

Capturing the Remote Audience

Every communicator deals with a remote audience at one point or another, and most find it a challenging experience. And, I get asked for easy tips to improve this experience all the time.

But, there is no simple solution. Remote communication is a hard medium, and it takes more effort to achieve the same level of effectiveness. Communicators may initially choose the remote format as an "easy way out," because they can read their notes and avoid the pressure of standing in front of a group. While that's true, the interest level and attention span of the listeners diminishes as well. The remote listener may be the toughest audience you ever face.

The listeners are now the invisible audience and it's really no wonder that they are so hard to engage. While the cancellation rate for in-person meetings typically hovers around 10%, mediums like webinars and all-hands calls average a 40-50% no-show rate from confirmed participants. And even the ones that do dial-in or log-on, are not automatically present.

Whenever I ask a group for a show of hands of people who give 100% of their attention to a remote presentation, not a single hand is raised. It's just too tempting to multitask when you're invisible. As listeners, we also tend to lower our expectations of what we will get out of remote presentations.

So, before the communicator even gets started, they're faced with an audience whose initial interest and attention are waning.

Here's a common situation.

Anika has scheduled a one-hour call with a group of people who will draft a timeline for a major project she is leading. In the discussion, she plans to get agreement on key milestones for the project and buy-in on deliverables. She's sitting at the front of an empty conference table talking remotely to a group of people who may as well have their backs turned to her. She can't see them, so she has no idea if they are engaged in the presentation or even in the same room as their computers.

Anika's setting is not ideal, but remote communication is often the only feasible option if people are spread around the globe or schedules and travel plans are impossible to coordinate. It saves time and money to pull people together remotely.

For the communicator, the approach has to adjust to connect with this audience. The critical skills are to learn how to keep the focus narrow, to require participation and to deliver specific takeaways from every call.

I call these skills the 3 P's of remote meetings:

Preparation:

When presenters are dealing with an unfocused audience, they need to be crystal clear about the objective of the presentation and what they're trying to accomplish. This often calls for more preparation and sending out advance agendas so that listeners understand their role in the presentation.

Keep the objective narrow. Most people are accustomed to ineffective remote conversations, so they'll be skeptical at first. The presenter needs to earn their attention, and they'll get it by setting realistic goals for the call and reaching those goals on every call.

So, consider Anika's example again. She's scheduled an hour-long meeting to draft the timeline of a major project, get agreement on key milestones for the project and buy-in on deliverables. In a remote meeting, she can't accomplish both. She would be better off scheduling two thirty-minute calls and setting only one objective for each call.

Participation:

If someone is leading a lot of remote calls, they'll need to focus on facilitation skills and learn how to solicit verbal responses to keep all participants involved. Even though people are poor listeners on the phone, most people would rather participate than waste valuable time listening half-heartedly. Multi-tasking is a learned behavior and one that can engage listeners with a little effort. Early in the call, a presenter should signal to a group that they expect their full participation and that they plan to call on them throughout the discussion.

I coach communicators to use polling or easy response questions at the start of the call to give everyone a "voice." This can quickly engage all the listeners and start everyone on equal footing with the discussion. Polling means asking for a one word or phrase response to a question. This helps the leader read the audience and gauge their initial perspectives on the topic.

In Anika's case, she could begin the call by asking each participant to weigh in on the following question:

"Based on your role in this initiative, are you most comfortable with a timeframe of three months, four months, or six months?" By asking each person on the call to respond with three, four, or six, Anika will quickly get a pulse on where the most pressure will be for the project and whose challenges need to be addressed first.

Calls that engage all listeners in conversation within the first 2–3 minutes yield higher participation overall. Presenters should construct an agenda that encourages input throughout the call, and continue to engage participants with questions and gauge their reactions. Presenters should also vary the way that they pose the questions, using fill-in-the-blank statements, open-ended questions, or "top three" lists.

Presence:

It can be challenging for remote participants to stay engaged when 55% of their impression is normally shaped by body language. Video adds significant advantage to a remote setting, and I encourage all communicators to use videoconferencing when they have the ability to do so.

When the audience can't see a presenter, they can only engage by hearing them. So while the voice accounts for 38% of an audience's initial impression of a live communicator, it shifts to 85% when we're only listening to them. That puts a lot of pressure on the voice to express confidence and commitment to lead the discussion.

The voice elements covered in Chapter 23 are still relevant; there's just more pressure to excel at them. It takes more articulation to communicate remotely, because you are often trying to pull the listener's attention back into the call rather than simply keeping them involved. It takes practice—and coaching—to learn how to include enough variety, pace, and energy to the voice to sustain a remote presentation. Think of a radio DJ or an audio book—the role of the voice is expanded and much more demanding.

The scenario suggests that Anika is sitting right at the front of a conference room, which may mean that she's right on top of a device that is transmitting the meeting. She would do better to position herself at least three feet away from the device so that her voice can travel forward to the device rather than down into it. If she has the benefit of a teleconference setting, she should also be talking forward to people on the screen rather than looking down into a computer.

Remote calls can be effective if you set narrow objectives, drive participation, and leverage your voice effectively. The invisible audience is less invested in remote calls, but with the right tools and intention, you can move them from low expectations to active participation.

28

The Wrap Up

As the book comes to a close, I want to circle back to where we started and the three-step formula:

Storylines, Stories, and Storytellers.

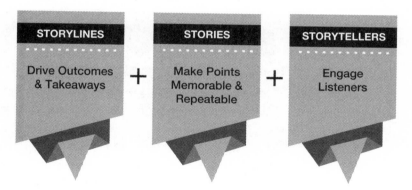

As I mentioned at the pivot point, the elements of the storyline will always lead a listener to a destination. There's a science to clear communication and the first half of the book gave you the tools and steps to organize effective storylines. Clarity helps a listener understand your point and reach a clear takeaway with you.

But stories are both a science and an art. As you saw in the stories section, there are elements of a story that follow a template just like the storyline and there are also elements that are more about the emotion of the story and the risks of the storyteller. There's a little magic to telling a story well and investing in the listener enough to make your point memorable and repeatable.

When all three elements work together, you have a compelling communicator that colleagues remember, employees follow and listeners value. It isn't an easy skill to develop, but it is a valuable one. And it's why I've spent my career trying to teach the science and unlock the magic of these communication components.

And it seems a perfect way to close the book would be to share a part of my story and how I discovered the magic of storytelling.

Remember the scene at the opening of this book? The conference with a thousand listeners waiting to hear a keynote address? In my story, the listeners aren't there yet. It's the day before the conference opening and the lead presenters are coming into the large ballroom for their rehearsals.

The rehearsal is mostly about the bells and whistles. It helps a production crew set staging and lights and sound checks, entrances and exits. Sometimes it's about catching a stumbling point for a presenter.

I was there as one of several resources who had supported the development of the conference, and it was quite a conference. Most members of the executive team would present over the course of three days. I was there to support a young woman—a client of mine—a lot like the manager in Chapter 1. She had worked on her storyline and her personal style with me, and she had become an authentic and engaging storyteller.

The story didn't go quite as I told it in Chapter 1, but I've seen many conference openings that were very much that way. At this particular conference, the magic of the storyteller (one of my clients) actually showed up in the rehearsal phase, and the CEO noticed it. He rehearsed after my client, and his rehearsal didn't go as well as hers.

There was a team of about six people with him including speechwriters, a speech coach, and the producer of the event. As he ran through his keynote, everything seemed to be going wrong. He couldn't read the teleprompter, he stumbled over his words, and he seemed very agitated by the whole experience. They'd take breaks and rewrite parts of the speech or reset the teleprompter, but nothing improved.

As a less "seasoned" coach in the back of the ballroom, I was fascinated by this and stayed to see how it would be resolved. It seemed to me that he was stumbling with a story his team wanted him to tell.

And, the more he worked at it, the worse it got. The producer was checking his watch, and the speechwriters were chewing the end of their pens. He was getting input from too many people. Their feedback wasn't helping and finally, he stormed off the stage and huddled with his speech coach.

Then, something surprising happened. He called the young manager up on the stage. Their conversation was quiet enough that no one else could hear, but I saw them glancing in my direction. He stepped to the front of the stage and called me out by name. "Sally, have you been working with Sarah?"

I stood up and responded that I had.

His entire team turned around to see who he was talking to in the back of the ballroom. He said, "Sarah says that you're the best coach here, and you've really helped her learn how to engage an audience. Do you think you can improve what my team has done?"

This was a clear no-win situation. This leader was practically a household name, and anyone in my position would be flattered to work with him. But not a single person at the front of that room thought that was a good idea. So, I said nothing thinking it might have been a rhetorical question he was using to make a point to his team rather than to engage with me.

But, he called out to me again and insisted that I come up on the stage with him. It felt like the last mile walking to the front of that ballroom and onto that stage with all eyes on me. And while I should have been intimidated by the man and the situation, I actually did know what was wrong.

So, I told him.

"You have a good story, but it's not your story. When you try to tell the story, there's no energy behind your words. It doesn't feel as if you've lived the story and as a listener, I don't believe you."

There may have been a gasp or two from his team. I'm sure there was shock because I would later learn that no one gave him honest feedback like that. But, he heard it. And he asked me if I could fix it.

We walked off stage, sat down in the back, and talked about stories. I got to know him a little and the topic he was planning to address with his team. It became an interview as I dug a little deeper to understand what he wanted the audience to feel and what his own experiences were around the topic. In a few hours, we had uncovered a story that seemed to suit him.

He didn't invite me to the rescheduled rehearsal that evening, and I was glad to be out from under the pressure his team felt that day. But he did invite me to every rehearsal after that. I wrote for him and with him and kept him focused on sharing himself with every audience. I became his coach, and we worked on his style, his stories, and his ability to be vulnerable with an audience.

I followed him to four different companies and worked with his internal teams to deliver compelling storylines and a more engaging style on every stage. As he expanded companies and experiences, he would send me thoughts to weave into his future speeches. His subject line always read, "Add this to my stories." And, I did the adding for twenty years.

It's my story about where I saw the magic of storytelling transform a communicator, and over time, I helped the communicator engage every listener with a story.

And, this is where I hope that your story will pick up. Whether you're leading a company or just getting started in one, you can become a master storyteller. I believe in the power of stories, and I believe stories are within every communicator. I hope that you'll find the stories within you.

Appendix
Survey Results

Survey Administered by The Bantam Group
December 2016- January 2017

Setting expectations for the listener prior to presentations is an opportunity.

60% 👥👥👥👥👥

Listeners are often unsure of...

- What they will be asked to do with the content.
- What, if anything, they need to prepare/be prepared to comment on.

30% 👥👥👥👥👥

Listeners are unsure of...

- Why they have been invited.
- What the presentation topic is.
- Who the presenter will be.

Presentation Impact

Attending meaningful presentations is hit or miss. Half of the listeners say presentations are...

50% rarely memorable.

50% frequently too long.

46% rarely entertaining or enjoyable.

45% a waste of time at least half the time.

Listeners prefer a presenter who is a great storyteller – one who uses stories to make a point – over one who is brief, knowledgeable or factual. Yet...

80% listeners say presenters don't often use stories, and...

60% say few presenters are good storytellers.

Memorable Stories

According to listeners...

 22% frequently hear memorable stories.

Two things would make stories memorable...

- If the presenter were a better storyteller.

- If the story aligned better with the topic.

Stories are repeated even less often...

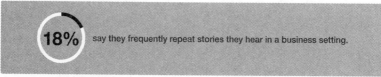

18% say they frequently repeat stories they hear in a business setting.

Reasons Stories Are Not Repeatable
• TOP 3 •

1. Can't connect with the story.

2. Story is too long.

3. Topic/story doesn't apply to anything I do.

Things That Make Stories Repeatable
• TOP 3 •

1. Being able to connect with a person/situation.

2. Storyteller's emotions.

3. Surprises/twists in the story.

Presentations are a fact of business life – everyone has to attend them.

92% attend presentations.

33% attend (on average) more than one presentation a week.

When it comes to applying what listeners hear/learn...

45% rarely re-tell a story they hear in a presentation.

33% are convinced of a new way to think about a topic.

32% rarely incorporate learnings into their own presentations.

28% hear things they want to tell others.

27% are inspired to do something.

Listeners suggest the most important things about being a good storyteller are...

 making the audience think.

 entertaining the audience.

Finally, listeners say the types of stories that have the most impact are stories about a...

79% personal experience.

48% business experience.

Three primary reasons stories are not told more often...

62% are not confident storytellers.

54% say it's just not easy.

36% don't have enough stories to tell (but they're good storytellers!).

However, among those who make presentations...

30% frequently tell stories to try and make a point in business, while

40% rate their storytelling skills as better than others.

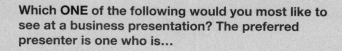

Which ONE of the following would you most like to see at a business presentation? The preferred presenter is one who is...

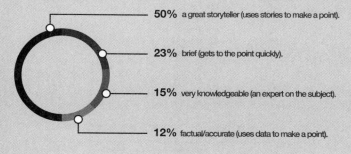

50% a great storyteller (uses stories to make a point).

23% brief (gets to the point quickly).

15% very knowledgeable (an expert on the subject).

12% factual/accurate (uses data to make a point).

How often do presenters you see tell stories to make a point?

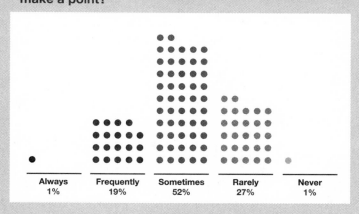

Always	Frequently	Sometimes	Rarely	Never
1%	19%	52%	27%	1%

How often are the stories you hear at presentations memorable – meaning, you can remember them for some time after the presentation?

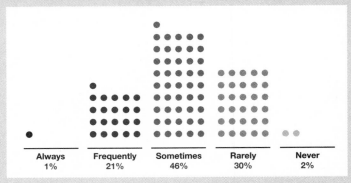

Always	Frequently	Sometimes	Rarely	Never
1%	21%	46%	30%	2%

How often do you repeat the stories you hear in a presentation – either in a conversation, a meeting or in a presentation you are given?

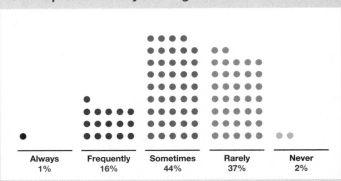

Always	Frequently	Sometimes	Rarely	Never
1%	16%	44%	37%	2%

Which of the following makes a story repeatable?

76% If I can connect with a person or a situation described in the story.

68% The emotions of the storyteller (e.g., laughter, anger, etc.).

53% Surprises or twists in the story.

44% The length of the story (not too long).

40% Visual images (e.g., pictures, photos, video, etc.).

33% Specific details about a person, place or thing (e.g., he wore this big red hat to every meeting).

8% Audio (e.g., songs, tunes, etc.).

Why aren't some stories repeatable for you?

74% I couldn't connect with the story.

61% The story was too long.

57% The topic/story does not apply to anything I do.

36% Didn't like the story.

36% Everyone has already heard that story.

7% Other.

How often do you tell stories to make a point – either in a business conversation, meeting or presentation?

Always	Frequently	Sometimes	Rarely	Never
3%	30%	48%	17%	2%

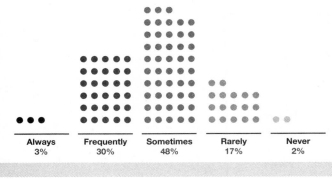

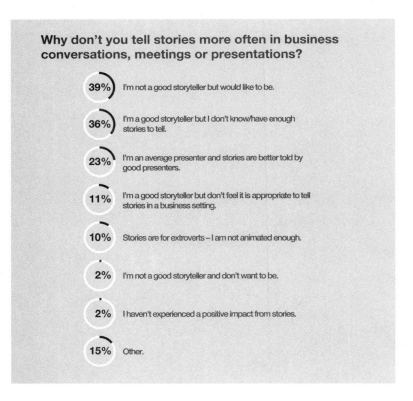

Why don't you tell stories more often in business conversations, meetings or presentations?

39% I'm not a good storyteller but would like to be.

36% I'm a good storyteller but I don't know/have enough stories to tell.

23% I'm an average presenter and stories are better told by good presenters.

11% I'm a good storyteller but don't feel it is appropriate to tell stories in a business setting.

10% Stories are for extroverts – I am not animated enough.

2% I'm not a good storyteller and don't want to be.

2% I haven't experienced a positive impact from stories.

15% Other.

Resources

Framework for Organizing Ideas

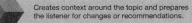

SITUATION: The Listener Perspective — Creates context around the topic and prepares the listener for changes or recommendations.

What occurred and why did it occur?
- External factors that impacted outcomes
- Internal implications from trends
- Identifies opportunity or gap
- What should we do next?

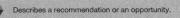

SOLUTION: Your Perspective — Describes a recommendation or an opportunity.

How do we resolve or leverage it?
- Answers the issues set up in the Situation
- Specific activity or recommendation
- Details or tactics

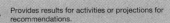

IMPACT/NEXT STEPS: Proof Points — Provides results for activities or projections for recommendations.

When will we see impact?
- Answers the Message
- Expected outcomes or projections
- Proven results/Impact
- Starting point/Next Step

CURRENT STATE

MESSAGE
⌄
SITUATION
⌄
SOLUTION
⌄
IMPACT/NEXT STEP

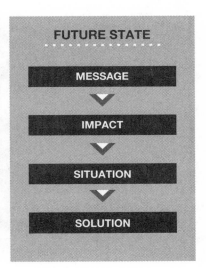

FUTURE STATE

MESSAGE
⌄
IMPACT
⌄
SITUATION
⌄
SOLUTION

221

Build the Experience Story

1 **Set the Stage.**
Start with context that helps the audience imagine the situation.

2 **Introduce the Point of Conflict.**
You want your audience to relate to the main character and to see themselves as the person you are describing.

3 **Solve the Problem.**
Tell how the conflict is resolved.

4 **End with Impact.**
Whether the story has a happy ending or a surprise ending, it needs to have impact.

5 **Wrap Up.**
Tie the ending back to the concept/message you wanted to introduce.

Build the Data Story

1 **Set the Stage.**
State the question an audience might have about the data.

2 **Introduce Insights.**
Share your insights and observations.

3 **Hypothesis from Insights.**
Tell the audience what you conclude as a result.

4 **Options/Recommendations.**
Offer options the audience might consider based on the hypothesis.

5 **Wrap Up.**
Complete the story by referring back to the initial question.

222

OPENING _____

MESSAGE   If you (do this/your goal), you will (get this/listener's benefit).

_____

_____

OVERVIEW OF
FRAMEWORK   Preview the flow of the presentation by introducing the framework.

    SITUATION _____

    SOLUTION _____

    IMPACT _____

SITUATION   Describe the conditions that exist or the problems that need to be solved.

    EXTERNAL   What's driving change?
    PERSPECTIVE   *Marketplace, Competitors, Best Practices.*

_____

_____

_____

    INTERNAL   How has your company thought about the topic in the past?
    PERSPECTIVE   *Your Company's Interest in the Topic.*

_____

_____

    SPECIFIC   What has your company done around the topic and where you are today?
    PROGRAMS   *Current Views, Programs, or Specifics: Gaps/Examples/Pilots in*
    OR INITIATIVES   *Your Company.*

_____

_____

_____

    WHAT I'M   How can issues be resolved?
    SOLVING FOR

_____

_____

_____

223

SOLUTION   Describes how the problem or issue will be solved.

_____

_____

_____

_____

_____

_____

_____

_____

IMPACT/   Provides the measurement of results and/or the next steps for future
NEXTSTEPS course of action.

_____

_____

_____

_____

_____

_____

_____

_____

SUMMARY   _____

_____

_____

_____

CALL FOR QUESTIONS

CLOSING   _____

_____

_____